GOD'S
UNIVERSITY

A CURRICULUM ON SPIRITUAL MATURITY
MODELED ON THE LIFE OF ELIJAH

GOD'S
UNIVERSITY

A CURRICULUM ON SPIRITUAL MATURITY
MODELED ON THE LIFE OF ELIJAH

EDWARD C. MORRIS

Courier Publishing, Greenville, SC

God's University: A Curriculum on Spiritual Maturity Modeled on the Life of Elijah

ISBN: 978-1-955295-32-1

Courier Publishing
100 Manly Street
Greenville, South Carolina 29601
www.courierpublishing.com

PRINTED IN THE UNITED STATES OF AMERICA.

This book is dedicated to my dear wife, Brenda Lee. Without her encouraging support and prayers, I could not have completed this book.

In Praise of *God's University*

God's University by Edward Morris is a unique approach to understanding how the Bible illuminates the lessons of spiritual maturity. These lessons of spiritual growth are learned through the willingness to trust our Lord in the challenges of life.

Elijah's lessons of spiritual growth were not without their share of difficulties and failures. Mr. Morris takes us through the biblical lessons of how the Lord enabled, encouraged and emboldened the prophet.

The prophet learned, like all of us who enroll in God's University, that by putting our faith and trust in His promises, spiritual growth is assured and that graduation has already been secured.

André Thornton
Author, speaker, entrepreneur
Retired All Star Major League Baseball player

Contents

Foreword.. 11

Acknowledgments 13

Preface.. 15

Introduction 17

Class 101: The Brook at Cherith
(Enrolling the Freshmen)..................................... 23

Class 102: Zarephath
(Second Semester).. 43

Class 201: Fire at Mt. Carmel
(Examination Time).. 63

Class 202: Mt. Horeb
(Depression)... 83

Class 301: The Vineyard
(Off-Campus Teaching)....................................... 101

Class 302: The Hill
(Reflections of College) 115

Class 401: Fire from Heaven
(Graduation) 129

Appendix 139

Biography.. 143

Endnotes... 145

Foreword

Edward Morris is a successful entrepreneur in the chemical supply industry. As an African-American, he navigated the complexities of technology, science, and processes to achieve the ultimate success of growing a thriving business as a "small fish in a large pond" of chemical suppliers.

In his role as chief operating officer for his boutique chemical plant, he exercised every principle listed in this book, where he showcases the lessons learned from the life of the prophet Elijah.

Edward's greatest contribution to God, who empowered him to accomplish these great feats, has been his commitment to live out and share these *God's University* principles as a husband, father, mentor, friend, and teacher.

Through the lessons presented in this book, you will gain insight into how a godly man can exercise the biblical direction and mandate presented in John 3:30: "He must increase, but I must decrease" (KJV) while growing and sustaining a thriving business in a marketplace that is in chaos.

I recommend that you read and apply the lessons Edward Morris has outlined in *God's University*.

Donald Darnell Harper
CEO/CFO of Harper & Harper HR & OD Consultants
Author, Blessed is the Man

Acknowledgments

Whenever God gives a person a specific assignment, He also provides the individual with the help they need. For me, that help came in the presence of two dear friends: Linda Stokes Smith and Bob Zeller.

Linda provided excellent commentary and editorial assistance over the many months I worked on this book. Her multiple hours of consulting and reviewing were necessary, and I will always treasure her contributions.

I have been blessed to have Bob Zeller as a friend for many years. Bob has multiple skills which he constantly uses in his service to God. He is a tireless worker, and his help authoring this book was instrumental.

In my opinion, Linda and Bob are students at God's University and will one day be honor graduates.

Preface

This book studies the many trials and learning experiences committed Christians will undergo as they develop and mature in spiritual growth. It centers primarily on the recorded history of the prophet Elijah and follows his journey as God develops the prophet's faith.

We could study many godly people as models in our pursuit of spiritual maturity in addition to Elijah. Abraham, Moses, Daniel, and David are also worth investigating, so why choose Elijah?

There are multiple reasons for selecting Elijah. First, Elijah established the pattern or template for all the classical prophets of the Old Testament. Elijah also appeared in Israel's history at a critical time when the nation was heavily involved in idolatry. Israel needed a quick rebuke before God rendered a final and fatal judgment. Such warnings demand much attention in the Elijah story as recorded in 1 and 2 Kings.

Further, Elijah's narrative occurs in both the Old and New Testaments. In the New Testament, Elijah is identified as a type of John the Baptist in all three of the Synoptic Gospels: Matthew, Mark, and Luke. In addition, Elijah appeared with Moses and Jesus on the Mount of Transfiguration, and Elijah is also mentioned in the book of James as a man of prayer. In total, Elijah is mentioned twenty-eight times in the New Testament.

However, I chose Elijah because James 5:17 states, "Elijah is a man with a nature like ours." In studying Elijah, we are privy to the many emotions he encounters in his journeys. We learn of his joy, comfort, humor, sorrow, solace, fear, loneliness, discouragement, and despair. Such emotions are universal, so we can all profit from studying Elijah's life and how God can use our feelings and situations to develop and mature us.

Since the Bible provides many valuable insights for all Christians, the lessons and biblical truths learned by Elijah can also teach us. We can apply the knowledge gained by Elijah to our lives as we experience our own trials and difficulties.

I have categorized these teachings into a format typical for a curriculum one may encounter as a student enrolled in a college or university. I hope these teachings will benefit all who wish to graduate from God's University and receive a "well done" diploma.

Introduction

The Elijah narrative is fascinating. What is readily captivating is his appearance, courage, devotion, miraculous powers, and final exit from earth. Examples of his human frailty and despair are interspersed in the text — as well as illustrations of his faith, obedience, perseverance, and sacrifice.

We know little about Elijah's ancestry and even less about his social and academic credentials, but we do know two facts. First, Elijah was from the town of Tishbe and the region of Gilead — a possible reference to his birthplace. Gilead today is a historical region in the western area of modern-day Jordan. Second, the name Elijah means "Yahweh is my god." Having been given such a name by his parents could possibly indicate the type of upbringing Elijah received at an early age. Beyond these limited facts, the rest of Elijah's past is unknown.

Elijah suddenly and without introduction appears on the biblical scene in 1 Kings 17:1 by speaking directly to King Ahab: "Now Elijah the Tishbite, who was of the settlers of Gilead, said to Ahab …" Elijah was a man who was highly favored by God and considered to be one of the greatest, if not the greatest, of Israel's Old Testament prophets.

Often in Scripture, we find an absence of background knowledge about significant biblical figures. For example, a detailed physical description of our Lord Jesus might be interesting. Things such as how tall He was or what color His eyes were?

We might also like to know more about the apostle Paul's thorn in the flesh. In 2 Corinthians 12:7, we read, "Because of the surpassing greatness of the revelation, for this reason, to keep me from exalting myself, there was given me a thorn in the flesh, a messenger of Satan to torment me — to keep me from exalting myself!"

But would such knowledge benefit us? In cases like these and with Elijah, God does not want us to concentrate too greatly on minor and unimportant details. Instead, the Lord wants us to understand the essential lessons specific biblical figures can teach us.

Nevertheless, what specifically about Elijah fascinates those who read about his exploits? Why is he held in such high regard? Why do the New Testament writers refer to him as the fulfillment of prophecy and a person worth emulating? Why did God so richly favor him? While no human can ever fully comprehend the mind of God, we can still wonder and seek answers to such questions.

I wrote this book to guide today's developing Christians by providing some insights into Elijah's faith maturation. I also constructed it around the seven major events of Elijah's life. Within these events are educational lessons we can apply universally to all Christians. I categorize these seven events as seven unique classrooms in which God taught and tested Elijah. I hope the lessons Elijah learned, when properly examined and applied, will help us grow in our faith and glorify our Lord and Savior, Jesus Christ.

The information presented here is based on researching numerous books and articles about Elijah and interviews with prominent theologians. Additionally, I have drawn from my personal experiences. I also hope and pray that we will receive the same blessings as Elijah by finishing our lives with God's power fully impacting our lives. I am not implying that we can all experience the rapture of a fiery chariot and a whirlwind rise to Heaven like Elijah.

However, we can grow closer to our Lord by learning and understanding the spiritual lessons and testing God gave to His servant. With a thorough knowledge of such universal spiritual lessons, we can recognize when we are being tested and then successfully apply that knowledge. This will enable us to navigate the trials and adversities we may experience in own providential classrooms. We can also enjoy the many wonderful blessings God offers His children who have learned to trust and obey Him as Elijah did.

This book is not a full biography of Elijah. Neither is it a personalized commentary on each of the recorded works he performed. Instead, this book explores the theological theme and structure of the Elijah narrative based on the Elijah narrative recorded from 1 Kings 17 through 2 Kings 2. Chapters 20 and 22 of 1 Kings do not contain any of the Elijah narratives and therefore I do not discuss them.

Finally, for Christians who sincerely want to mature in their faith, I pray this book will help them achieve the result of hearing the words from our heavenly Savior, "Well done, good and faithful servant" (Matthew 25:23 ESV).

GOD'S
UNIVERSITY

A CURRICULUM ON SPIRITUAL MATURITY
MODELED ON THE LIFE OF ELIJAH

CLASS 101
The Brook at Cherith

(Enrolling the Freshmen)

"Now Elijah the Tishbite, who was of the settlers of Gilead, said to Ahab, 'As the LORD, the God of Israel lives, before whom I stand, surely there shall be neither dew nor rain these years, except by my word.' The word of the LORD came to him, saying, 'Go away from here and turn eastward, and hide yourself by the brook Cherith, which is east of the Jordan. It shall be that you will drink of the brook, and I have commanded the ravens to provide for you there.' So he went and did according to the word of the LORD, for he went and lived by the brook Cherith, which is east of the Jordan. The ravens brought him bread and meat in the morning and bread and meat in the evening, and he would drink from the brook. It happened after a while that the brook dried up, because there was no rain in the land" (1 Kings 17:1–7).

God commissioned Elijah to announce an unpleasant message to a pagan king. Typically, when a person has a king for his audience, they refrain from saying anything distasteful. The danger for Elijah was that his announcement might not be well received and could be perilous. Therefore, the first action for a student of God is to be valiant and committed to the initial orders the Almighty gave.

The prophet Elijah was given information directly from God. Elijah appeared before King Ahab and boldly announced that he was not speaking his own words but the words of God: "As the LORD, the God of Israel lives, before whom I stand . . ." The prophet then announces that there would be "neither dew nor rain these years, except by my word" (1 Kings 17:1).

In Class 101, the objective is to ascertain our current courage and commitment level for fulfilling God's commands. This is an imperative position that students must have if they want to be a student at God's University. I refer to it as "the enrollment of the freshman."

After delivering that catastrophic and unwelcome message, God commanded Elijah to travel eastward to a small brook known as Cherith, located east of the Jordan River. Elijah was to hide, but God promised him water from the brook and food from ravens (1 Kings 17:3–4).

Cherith was in the wilderness and was a place of utter isolation. Elijah was in a place of total solitude. The Cherith location is the first of the seven classrooms in which God will instruct His servant Elijah as he grows in the divine faith.

Why did God remove Elijah so entirely from all civilization? Why did God instruct him to hide? The popular and most obvious answer is that it was for Elijah's physical protection and safety. Elijah had declared a severe drought. No rain would fall unless he desired it. By giving such a dire prophecy to King Ahab, a man who clearly did not honor God or His commands, Elijah announced a severe judgment on the king and his entire nation. As that prophecy unfolded, many people became angry with Elijah. Others might praise those who bring good news, but they condemn those who bring bad news. Elijah, merely the messenger who delivered God's Word, would have become a marked man and placed his life in jeopardy.

But would Elijah's life really have been in great peril? Could not Almighty God have protected him from the king and the people? Recall 1 Kings 18:4, which recounts how Obadiah saved one hundred prophets from the murderous Queen Jezebel. Just as God protected those prophets from Jezebel, He could have done the same for Elijah. And what about the many other believers God has protected from danger throughout the centuries?

Scripture is replete with narratives that speak of God's divine protection. Abraham, Joseph, Job, and David are just a few of those whom God has sheltered from deadly adversaries. The book of Esther even describes how God moved in supernatural ways to deliver His entire nation from the evil of its enemies.

I suggest Elijah's removal to Cherith was not primarily for his physical protection but a sign He had finished speaking to the people. It was now time for them to respond by either repenting and accepting God or rejecting Him. Through Elijah's proclamation, God set forth the full power of His glory and sovereignty before the people. If they refused Him, God's judgment would fall.

When people turn away from God repeatedly, He is merciful and gracious. He gives them many opportunities to repent — but only for a time. God's patience is great, but it is not infinite. Eventually, God will let the people pursue whatever they desire, however disastrous it might be.

Amos wrote, "Behold, days are coming," declares the Lord God, "when I will send a famine on the land, not a famine for bread or a thirst for water, but rather for hearing the words of the Lord" (Amos 8:11).

God stopped Elijah from further preaching God's word because of the people's rebellious attitude. God instructed Elijah to leave them.

When examining the word "hide" (Strong's Concordance 5641) in 1 Kings 17:3, we find that it does not have the same meaning as when "hide" (Strong's Concordance 2247) is used in Joshua 6:17, 25 or 1 Kings 18:4, 13. Joshua 6, verses 17 and 25, refer to Rahab hiding the Israelite spies. 1 Kings 18, verses 4 and 13, refer to Obadiah hiding the Jewish prophets and sheltering them in a cave from Queen Jezebel.

But the hiding of Elijah, as recorded in 1 Kings 17:3, uses the Hebrew root word that pertains to being physically absent or apart. It was not simply a concealment to avoid being discovered by those around him. God commanded Elijah to leave that place and become absent from the nation's influence . . . to be hidden, so he was not known.

God wants us to remove ourselves from the negative influences of our ungodly world. But God is not advocating a wholly monastic and isolationist path. Instead, He wants us to shield ourselves from our world's socialized charm of demonic temptation. God wants His servants to avoid being influenced by the debauchery of today's societal norms. We must be in the world but not of the world.

We can learn a special lesson from Elijah's stay at Cherith Brook. Alone in the wilderness, Elijah was helpless and without any resources. He had no provisions, food, water, or shelter. But God gave him water from the brook and had ravens bring him bread and meat. To survive, Elijah relied entirely on God. He had no choice.

Elijah learned to adapt to his unique situation and

accept the sustenance God provided. Being fed with food delivered by ravens, carrion eaters themselves, required an unusual degree of acceptance on Elijah's part. Additionally, receiving water from a ground-running brook rather than a well was unconventional. Relying on such unconventional food and water supplies for his survival developed great trust and humility in Elijah.

The two virtues of trust and humility should also be significant features of every Christian's character. At any moment, God might place us in a situation where we will be equally helpless. Circumstances may force us to depend on Him to deliver our needed support in unexpected and unique ways that make us uncomfortable. God may not always aid us as we expect or desire. God could have sent an angel to feed and care for Elijah. Later, He did as recorded in 1 Kings 19:5–6. Or, God could have had Obadiah come and feed Elijah. Jesus Himself was ministered to by angels during the forty days He spent in the wilderness (Mark 1:12).

But that was not God's plan for Elijah. Instead, God chose an unorthodox and unexpected method to aid His servant, yet one that fully met Elijah's needs. Compared to being cared for by an angel or Obadiah, Elijah may have enjoyed a more pleasant fate. One could argue that Elijah received a more delectable culinary diet. The angel and Obadiah provided only bread and water to those they served.

God, using birds as His instruments of grace, provided Elijah with meat and water, a good diet. When God satisfies our needs through unconventional methods, which we do not fully understand or expect, we may receive a greater blessing than the desired outcome.

The next lesson from the Cherith classroom concerns time. We do not know how long Elijah stayed at the brook. 1 Kings 17:7 simply states that "after a while . . . the brook dried up." Elijah probably remained there for an extended time, perhaps a year or longer. We can assume the brook dried up gradually.

Why was Elijah there for so long? Elijah needed time to fully understand and appreciate the lessons God wanted to teach him. The lessons Elijah learned in the Cherith classroom are foundational and relate to the basics of the faith. God was not about to send His prophet into the world again until He had prepared him.

God is in no hurry to advance us if we need more

time to learn and appreciate His lessons. God's curriculum is cumulative. We must learn each lesson and apply it to our lives before advancing. This helps us avoid impatience and frustration. God moves us ahead by His timetable, not ours.

While Elijah was alone in Cherith, God was with him, teaching him needed lessons. Recall the words of Isaiah 50:4b, "He awakens Me morning by morning, He awakens My ear to listen as a disciple."

Too often, we feel we have learned a particular lesson and are ready immediately to pursue our spiritual maturation. We are sure now is the time to move beyond our current situation and advance in our studies. We are prepared to take the next step, or so we think. Yet, God often keeps us where we are, serving and studying in the same location or situation. Such a perceived stagnation can be frustrating.

After a time, Elijah probably wanted to leave that isolated environment and know how his nation was progressing. While he was undoubtedly grateful for God's providential sustenance, Elijah probably longed to return to society and resume his active life. After all, Elijah's life at the brook Cherith was not exciting. There would have been little change in his daily routine, diet, or environmental setting. Boredom could have been a significant problem for Elijah. Additionally, we have a natural desire for human companionship. Despite any danger he might have faced, Elijah would have wanted to leave Cherith and move on to the next chapter of his life.

Despite our desire to advance, we must remember to trust in our Lord and know His timing is best, whether it agrees with ours. God has placed us in a particular location at a specific time for a reason.

We must also remember God is a jealous God. He wants us for His own. Sometimes, He wants us alone with Him so we can share in the love and fellowship of His beloved Son. At such times of solitude and quiet, we can hear and understand more about the Lord than at any other moment, just as Jesus illustrated.

The geographical location of the Cherith classroom is also essential. Cherith was near the Jordan River. A. W. Pink, in his excellent commentary on Elijah, writes, "Jordan marked the very limits of the land. Typically it spoke of death, and spiritual death now rested upon Israel."[1]

The Jordan River is where God demonstrated His strength to His people in the days of Joshua and performed many other miracles for His people. Elijah was in a place with a great spiritual legacy. Each day, he could look around and recall the many wonders God had performed.

God never instructs us to go to a specific place because of a whim or idle decision. The places He sends us are places where He intends to provide for us, refresh us, protect us, and communicate with us. From our frail and limited perspective, these places may not appear as the most desirable locations. But they are always the best places for us if we want to receive the many blessings He has in store for us. Although Israel was spiritually dying, Elijah was spiritually strengthened. His trust in and reliance on God grew daily.

The last lesson we can learn in the Cherith classroom addresses failing resources. Elijah's water source diminished daily, and he was in a life-threatening situation: "It happened after a while that the brook dried up, because there was no rain in the land" (1 Kings 17:7).

This distressing development resulted from the ongoing drought Elijah himself had foretold. But that did not comfort Elijah at this critical time. He may have wondered how he would survive.

Many times, after having obeyed God, we may also find ourselves in a similar situation. The resources God has provided in the past wane and disappear. Questions and worries cross our minds. Did we misread God's instruction? Have we sinned? Did God tell us to do this? Has He left us out to dry (no pun intended)?

The answer to each question is "No." Instead, we need to do what Elijah did: wait for new instructions and guidance from the Lord. God does not always reveal His complete design and intention all at once. He wants us to trust in and rely on Him in all situations. He wants our obedience, even with the limited information we may have. When and only when God determines the time has come for us to advance, He will reveal the next step.

Many commentators believe the drought did not begin until after Elijah had made his fateful prediction to King Ahab. However, we can propose an alternative theory if we examine the time periods mentioned in Scripture. In 1 Kings 17:1, Elijah prophesied to Ahab that there would be no rain. Later, in 1 Kings 18:1, we read: "Now it happened after many days that the word of the Lord came to Elijah in the third year, saying, 'Go show yourself to Ahab and I will send rain upon the earth.'" Compare that verse to the words of Jesus Christ when He spoke about Elijah and the drought in Luke 4:25. Jesus said, "There were many widows in Israel in the days of Elijah when the heavens were shut up three years and six months, when a great famine came over all the land."

Many commentators believe Elijah specified that the drought would last precisely three years and no longer. But a careful reading of Scripture does not support that interpretation. Elijah does not establish an exact time; he merely states, "there shall be no dew nor rain these years, except by my word." That is a consistent interpretation outlined in the King James Version, the New Kings James Version, the New American Standard Bible, and the English Standard Version. In the New International Version and the New Living Translation, Elijah says there would be no dew or rain during "the next few years." I believe a proper reading of Scripture does not support that Elijah specified a drought of three years.

For the sake of argument, let us assume Elijah predicted a three-year drought. But Jesus later stated the drought lasted for three years and six months. Is this a discrepancy? The only reasonable answer is that the drought had already begun six months before Elijah visited King Ahab. Elijah's announcement that the drought would continue for another three years would only have infuriated Ahab since the king and his people had already experienced a growing famine for six months.

As for Elijah, the prophecy probably enhanced and deepened his faith because he had prayed for such an event. Elijah may have relied on God's word in Deuteronomy 11:16–17, which declared that a divine drought would occur if Israel worshipped false gods. Now, Elijah could see firsthand that God was answering his prayers. Elijah's courage before the apostate king was magnified tremendously.

We can now construct a curriculum to account for the growth of Elijah's strength, maturity, and faith in God, which he learned in the Cherith classroom. Prayer is paramount. Despite being in a difficult environment and situation, Elijah remained in regular communication with God. Elijah was alone, and yet he was not alone. God was with him every moment. Elijah completely trusted God for his welfare and survival. And God met and satisfied Elijah's needs. Elijah's patience grew as he waited for God to reveal His plans. Elijah also learned the difficult lesson of humility. To succeed, he had to ask God to give him strength, not rely on his own skills and resources.

Insights for Reflection

Upon entering college, I recall several intense periods of sadness and loneliness. Leaving my family behind and entering a new environment with other students of varying cultures and backgrounds was challenging. Becoming familiar with and accepting a new dietary regime — no more of my dear mother's cooking — strange roommates, and unexpected experiences affected my education. I was thrust into a new world for which I was not fully prepared. It took me some time to adapt to my new surroundings and become comfortable.

God led Elijah into a situation he could never have imagined or prepared for. God sent Elijah out into to a physical environment of complete isolation that nevertheless somehow had miraculous food service to supernaturally meet his needs. It was a place where Elijah was completely alone without any human company. He was also utterly helpless. Elijah was totally dependent on God for his very survival.

As I read of Elijah's initial curriculum, I notice a similarity to my experiences as a young college freshman. Although college was not a lonely physical place or a desperate situation, the strangeness and loneliness resembled Elijah's. Such an environment focused my attention on what was really important and not just what I desired. Such a change did not occur quickly but took place over many months and during difficult circumstances. The changes we encounter will entail ongoing activity.

After graduation, I realized the need to become more devout in my Christian walk. Changes such as marriage, a new job, parenthood, geographic relocation, significant injuries, major illnesses, and physical aging all offered distractions to remove God from the forefront of my life. While I could cite many examples, one particular episode affected me. After graduating, I became employed with a major oil company for nine years. Then, believing I was following God's direction, I left to start my own business — a manufacturer's representative sales organization. This proved to be a successful move, and I enjoyed a profitable business for several years. My wife and I enjoyed the fruits of our labors, and life was sweet.

But one day, things quickly turned sour. Within a short time, our income dried up, much like the brook in Cherith. The peace I had enjoyed by following God's call to entrepreneurship changed into fearful anxiety. When our personal brook dries up after fully committing our lives to God's plan, we can be disheartened. We may question God and our trust in Him. Such trials may weaken our faith, but these temporary setbacks are not the end. God still has great plans for us.

This proved true for me. Later, God blessed me with a much larger chemical manufacturing plant. I went from being a sole employee to having more than fifty employees. God does not finish using us until our lives on earth are over. Trials are just the next step God may use as He matures us and ensures that we depend more on Him.

As God prepares us for growth and ministry, He may place us suddenly in strange situations where we are removed from all supporting resources, requiring our total dependence on Him. In these circumstances, our senses are sharpened to hearing and developing our faith in the Almighty.

As new Christians begin their walk of faith, they may experience initial joy, inner peace, and excitement. But this may be followed by an unsettling sense of isolation as they realize that not everyone shares their beliefs and joy. They may experience some hostility and even persecution from others, even from loved ones and those whom they thought were friends. The new believer may painfully discover the world will not welcome them with open arms.

As Jesus Himself stated, "If the world hates you, you know that it hated me before it hated you. If you were of the world, the world would love its own; but because you are not of the world, but I chose you out of the world, because of this the world hates you. Remember the word that I said to you, 'A slave is not greater than his master.' If they persecuted Me, they will also persecute you." (John 15:18–21).

The social circle of a new Christian might change drastically, causing a time of great pain and puzzlement. Old friends and loved ones may distance themselves, while Christians will befriend him. Though emotionally difficult, removing ourselves from the influence of negative individuals and past sinful practices is one of the many steps to spiritual maturity. The pain is real and must be recognized and addressed. But as a new creation in Christ — yet one still struggling in a fleshly body — the new believer must understand a sanctification process is occurring. The transition from following the world to Christ is never easy, but always necessary.

Questions

1. When God calls you to perform a task with perilous risks, do you think it is acceptable to doubt such a call? Why or why not?

2. How important is it for Christians to periodically isolate themselves from all major distractions and influences to prepare for godly obedience?

3. How difficult is it to wait on God for His next instruction? How did you overcome this struggle?

CLASS 102
Zarephath

(Second Semester)

"Then the word of the LORD came to him, saying, 'Arise, go to Zarephath, which belongs to Sidon, and stay there; behold, I have commanded a widow there to provide for you.' So he arose and went to Zarephath, and when he came to the gate of the city, behold, a widow was there gathering sticks; and he called to her and said, 'Please get me a little water in a jar, that I may drink.' As she was going to get [it], he called to her and said, 'Please bring me a piece of bread in your hand.' But she said, 'As the LORD your God lives, I have no bread, only a handful of flour in the bowl and a little oil in the jar; and behold, I am gathering a few sticks that I may go in and prepare for me and my son, that we may eat it and die.' Then Elijah said to her, 'Do not fear; go, do as you have said, but make me a little bread cake from it first and bring [it] out

to me, and afterward you may make [one] for yourself and for your son. For thus says the LORD God of Israel, The bowl of flour shall not be exhausted, nor shall the jar of oil be empty, until the day that the LORD sends rain on the face of the earth.' So she went and did according to the word of Elijah, and she and he and her household ate for [many] days. The bowl of flour was not exhausted nor did the jar of oil become empty, according to the word of the LORD which He spoke through Elijah. Now it came about after these things that the son of the woman, the mistress of the house, became sick; and his sickness was so severe that there was no breath left in him. So she said to Elijah, 'What do I have to do with you, O man of God? You have come to me to bring my iniquity to remembrance and to put my son to death!' He said to her, 'Give me your son.' Then he took him from her bosom and carried him up to the upper room where he was living, and laid him on his own bed. He called to the LORD and said, O LORD my God, have You also brought calamity to the widow with whom I am staying, by causing her son to die?' Then he stretched himself upon the child three times, and called to the LORD and said, 'O LORD my God, I pray You, let this child's life return to him.' The LORD heard the voice of Elijah, and the life of the child returned to him and he revived. Elijah took the child and brought him down from the upper room into the house and gave him to his mother; and Elijah said, 'See, your son is alive.' Then the woman said to Elijah, 'Now I know that you are a man of God and that the word of the LORD in your mouth is truth'" (1 Kings 17:8–24).

The objective of this class is to ascertain the student's level of belief (faith), trust (dependence), and prayer life when given a directive by God.

At this point, we see the importance of steadfast commitment and courage to obey God. God had tested Elijah's faith, trust, humility, and obedience. These areas concerning one's faith, commitment and communication with the Almighty will have a direct impact on the student's success towards fulfilling God's directive in his or her life.

Elijah completed Class 101 — the foundations of the faith and the most basic introductory course. Next, God taught Elijah the fundamental lessons of the Christian faith. It took some time, but Elijah learned to believe in the message God had called him to proclaim publicly and accept the direction God led him. Additionally, Elijah learned to accept what God provided for his physical survival. Finally, Elijah grew stronger spiritually while experiencing physical difficulties.

Elijah was now about to move on to his next classroom lesson. God will teach him to have even greater assurance, confidence, and trust in God during the most unusual and unexpected circumstances. Elijah will soon enter into a study of evangelism — persuading others to believe in God.

When we attend school at a college or university, the travel time between classes is typically short. The next class may be just down the hall or, at most, a ten-minute walk across campus. For Elijah, however, his next classroom was a greater distance. God told Elijah, "Arise, go to Zarephath, which belongs to Sidon, and stay there" (1 Kings 17:9a).

Zarephath was a long distance from Cherith. Elijah would have had to cross a desert and travel through a hostile land at night to avoid discovery. Then he entered an idolatrous city where God's people were not welcome. To further complicate his journey, God gave

Elijah the following word: "I have commanded a widow there to provide for you" (1 Kings 17:9b). God sent Elijah on a long and dangerous journey to a place where he knew no one, hoping to find an unnamed widow who would care for him. We might wonder what thoughts went through Elijah's mind as he traveled across Israel and then into enemy territory, where there was still a bounty on his head.

When we step out to follow God's command, we should expect opposition. Such obstructions can present themselves through negative thoughts placed there by our spiritual enemies. As Elijah traveled onward, demonic thoughts such as the following may have invaded his mind: How foolish can you get? Don't you know that the people in this city hate you and might torture or kill you for bringing this calamity down upon them? What about this widow that God told you about? If the townspeople don't kill you, she might. A dagger will be plunged into your heart while you sleep. Or she will poison you with the food she provides. How will you even know who she is or what she looks like? Is she a woman who will seduce you and your testimony first and then destroy you? Elijah, you are on your way to a fatal failure.

Such thoughts might have flooded Elijah's mind day after day and night after night. But despite whatever fears and doubts he may have had, Elijah kept traveling. Such perseverance and unwavering commitment strengthened Elijah's faith and obedience, even while he fended off Satan's undermining doubts. It has been said that if the Devil is not bothering us, then we are not bothering him.

Elijah eventually arrived at the gate of Zarephath. Immediately, he noticed a woman who might be the widow of whom God spoke. But how could he know? Elijah asked the woman for water, which was a precious commodity at that time. The woman agreed to get him some. Then, because God had told him that a widow would supply all his needs, Elijah requested a piece of bread. By doing to, he completed another act of obedience.

Elijah's first lesson entailed doing what God had commanded. We must follow suit. We may not understand His command, but we are to obey with confidence that He will provide. He sought out an unknown woman in a hostile land and trusted God to lead him to her. Elijah demonstrated great faith because the woman could have quickly reported him as a spy to the authorities.

The widow told Elijah she did not have much to share. She had no bread and only a little flour and oil. She did not even have enough for herself and her son. She planned for them to eat one last meal and then die. She did not believe she could meet Elijah's needs too.

But in addressing Elijah, the widow acknowledged her faith in the Lord: "As the LORD your God lives" (1 Kings 17:12). To find someone who would publicly claim that Yahweh was the one true God in such an idolatrous and evil place must have been a blessing for Elijah. Believers everywhere should look for similar encouragement when carrying out their assigned tasks.

The widow trusted Elijah and did what he requested, believing he was a man of God. Elijah told the widow to make bread for him, her, and her son. She obeys. "And she and he and her household ate for many days" (1 Kings 17:15).

As we obey God, we, too, need to seek those who have faith that can encourage us. We are not alone. Many Christians can help us in our faith journey, and we can also help them in return. The widow provided food, water, and godly companionship. God met all the needs of his obedient servant.

One question, however, entails how we should respond to tragedies that occur even when we are obeying God's direction. Both Elijah and the widow were obeying God and were under His protection. God blessed them with an unending source of flour and oil. But a tragedy occurred — the sudden death of the widow's son (1 Kings 17:17–24).

Elijah's attitude and behavior are noteworthy. When the widow's son died, she was understandably upset and angry. She had trusted Elijah, but what was the result? The widow lashed out at Elijah, blaming and condemning him for her son's death: "You have come to me to bring my iniquity to remembrance and to put my son to death" (1 Kings 17:18)! Despite receiving such harsh and accusatory words from the widow, Elijah did not respond in-kind. Instead, he silenced his tongue and held his peace. Instead, Elijah advised the woman to give her dead son to him.

The lesson for us involves remembering Elijah's calm response. He could have easily exploded in anger and stormed out, leaving the woman behind with her dead son. But he did not. He withstood the blows of an unfair attack and demonstrated self-control.

As Christians, we should duplicate Elijah's patience when difficult situations arise. When a friend attacks us unjustly, we should not become defensive and retaliate. Jesus' disciples panicked when a storm appeared on the Sea of Galilee and tossed their boat (Matthew 8:23–27). They lashed out at Jesus, accusing Him of not caring if they died. But Jesus ignored their attack and directed His attention to the problem. He never answered their false statements but let His actions speak for Him.

Unfortunate events we can neither expect nor control will occur. We cannot see the future, only react as events unfold. Those who unfairly blame us also watch our reaction. These times provide opportunities to demonstrate God's life-changing power. God may not grant us what He gave Elijah to address and correct our problems, but we can choose to act calmly, kindly, and obediently.

When facing these difficult and stressful circumstances, we need God's Spirit to give us verbal restraint. Elijah did not rail against the widow and walk away. Instead, he trusted God for the power to resolve the tragic situation.

Elijah's actions are instructive. First, he took the dead child from the mother and went to an isolated place without interruptions. Then, he took his problem directly to God. Finally, Elijah laid out the boy's body and verbally told God his complaint (1 Kings 17:19). Elijah prayed, "O Lord my God, have you also brought calamity to the widow with whom I am staying, by causing her son to die" (1 Kings 17:20)?

While we do not see full-blown doubt in Elijah's prayer, he did express confusion. Elijah did not openly question God, but he wondered why the evil of death came after he and the widow had obeyed God.

Elijah did not ask God why in his prayer. The why issue was none of Elijah's business. Nor is it the place of believers to always know, understand, and approve of God's ways. In times of tragedy, we often demand that God explain His actions. We feel we are somehow entitled to a full explanation. But why God acts as He does is none of our business. He alone is sovereign. Who are we to demand an answer from our Creator? God said, "For My thoughts are not your thoughts; nor are your ways My ways," declares the Lord. "For as the heavens are higher than the earth, so are My ways higher than your ways. And My thoughts than your thoughts" (Isaiah 55:8-9).

Our Sovereign God makes no mistakes, nor is He ever surprised by an unexpected and unforeseen event. When we ask God "Why," we are talking back to God and not respecting His proper authority (Romans 9:19–20).

This does not mean we should never seek an explanation or more information. There will always be events and situations that we will encounter and be at a loss for comprehension. Our Savior knows this, and at such times he provides us with his peace and comfort. Nevertheless, in our human efforts to seek answers, there exists the potential to hold God to a human standard of fairness.

We see an example of this in Habakkuk 1:1-17 and 2:1. Here we read where the prophet is seeking and explanation from God as to why God was allowing the wicked to prosper. This was a valid request from the prophet; nevertheless, he realized his questions were human-based and, as a result, expected to be reproved by God if He answered him. Habakkuk fully understood that he was a finite creature who was seeking an answer from the infinite Creator God.

But we must remember God is the supreme creator and that without faith, it is impossible to please him (Hebrews 11:6). We trust that God is perfect in His ways and can comfort us in times of strife and trial. Our task is to glorify God by trusting in His Word and obeying His commands. If God chooses to explain His actions and reveal His design, that is a beautiful blessing. But if He remains silent, we must continue to follow Him.

In Elijah's prayer, he called God "my God." Elijah came boldly before the throne of God's grace, knowing he was privileged to do so because he had a personal relationship with God. In 1 Kings 17:20, Elijah acknowledged God was in control and responsible for the boy's death. In the next verse, he attested that only God could bring the child back to life, then prayed, "O LORD my God, I pray You, let this child's life return to him." Elijah called on God to perform a miracle. Elijah requested a supernatural act that no human could have performed. Scripture does not previously record anyone asking God to perform such a powerful and amazing miracle.

Once again, we should note the tremendous faith Elijah demonstrated in this classroom. Elijah knew God could fulfill his request — no matter how incredible it may have appeared to anyone else.

When we pray, we should acknowledge God's power to fulfill any desire or need. We should come, acknowledging our intimate relationship with Him, His total sovereignty, and His infinite power. Our great God can grant any request we bring before Him, however impossible it may appear.

Also, notice how Elijah related to the dead son. The prophet stretched himself on the child, not one but three times (1 Kings 17:21). Elijah did not give up after just one time. He persevered, confident God would hear his prayer and respond favorably. We should be willing to commit ourselves entirely to the Lord and persevere in our requests.

A. W. Pink asked the following question: "Was this act indicative of [Elijah's] own affection for the child, and to show how deeply he was stirred by [the child's] death?"[2]

Elijah's prayer illustrated a personal commitment and a request for divine resuscitation. Many times during his life, Elijah witnessed God's miraculous power. We should also recall how many times God has moved miraculously in our lives. Sadly, we often forget the many blessings and miracles God has sent. A humble remembrance of past answered prayers is an important and indispensable tool for all Christians.

Let us review the lessons we have learned from Elijah's time in the Zarephath classroom. First, Elijah continued to exercise and build his faith. Second, Elijah practiced and strengthened his humility. Third, God repeatedly answered his prayers. Fourth, Elijah's protection was being maintained. Fifth, Elijah's courage and commitment remained intact and grew. Finally, God tested Elijah's patience.

God addressed and strengthened Elijah's fortitude and faith in the Zarephath classroom. God also taught Elijah how to reach out to others and deal with significant personal tragedies. In Elijah's next classroom, Mt. Carmel, we will see how God addressed the prophet's fearlessness.

Insights for Reflection

During my first year of college, I formed many new friendships. One friend whom I came to know well was a beautiful young girl. I quickly fell in love with her, and eventually, we married. Unfortunately, while we were close initially, we later drifted apart. Our relationship failed and remained broken for far too long. But God healed the fracture between us, and eventually, we formed a loving bond that remains strong today.

It is not uncommon for God to remove our enjoyment and pleasure for a season without any explanation. We may wonder why, but God alone is sovereign—a basic fact of our Christian faith. When we trust God, times of disappointment will bring us closer to Him, increasing our love for Him.

Elijah may have initially wondered why God would allow such a tragedy as the boy's death. It was inconsistent with God's blessings on Elijah and the widow before. What good could ever come from such adversity? Indeed, the widow had such thoughts, too. But God used the boy's death for His great purpose. Elijah witnessed a miracle and appreciated an amazing new level of God's demonstrated power. As for the widow, she was given the gift of God's love and compassion, and her faith was strengthened. She said, "Now I know that you are a man of God and that the word of the LORD in your mouth is truth" (1 Kings 17:24).

Many factors play a part in the spiritual maturing process. Like horticulture — which includes planting, watering, fertilizing, and pruning — the Christian needs nourishment, exhorting, and chastening for real spiritual growth. My own development has consisted of periods of isolation, in-depth study, unanswered prayer, and various illnesses. God is always at work to use our growth to help others.

I once experienced an event during my early faith journey that illustrates the above. My wife and I struggled with a significant illness early in our marriage. After ensuring that she would be adequately cared for, I took a retreat at a monastery for a time of reflection and solitude. It was winter, and the castle-like structure was quite cold. One day while praying, I felt a strong desire to walk outside. After walking for a considerable distance along a wooden pathway, I saw an old cabin that appeared vacant. Curiously, I knocked on the door, and it quickly opened. Inside was a desk that had a note requesting help. A young girl was ill and wanted anyone reading the note to offer a prayer for her. I knelt and prayed for this girl, knowing I would probably never meet her or see the outcome.

As I walked back, I reflected on what had occurred. God used me to pray for someone else, just as He had used others to pray for my wife. We are a community of believers. Sometimes, we may feel forgotten, but nothing is further from the truth. God is always at work on our behalf, which brings us great peace. He is compassionate and capable, even when we tend to think otherwise. Our faith can struggle and weaken, but our Savior is never weak and does not struggle.

The freshman Christian may discover that many events make no sense, but we cannot fully understand God's ways. We are finite beings. We may see the results of God's work, but we do not understand how or why God moved. God's workings are a mystery. This confusion is a phenomenon that may repeatedly occur during a believer's lifetime.

Classroom 102 also has a lesson for us to learn about pride and humility. It teaches us to show restraint and not retaliate when others accuse us unfairly. The widow accused Elijah of being responsible for her guilt and her child's death. Elijah did not respond to either of these accusations.

In Mark 4:38, the disciples accused Jesus of not caring that they were about to drown. Jesus, like Elijah, did not respond to such undeserved criticism. Instead, Jesus directed His focus and skills toward the more pressing problem.

How we respond to these God moments will determine how much we grow and bring us nearer to our graduation day.

Questions

1. Can you identify an area of trust you would have difficulty in if you felt God was asking you to depend solely upon Him?

2. How does the power of prayer affect your life? Give specific examples.

3. When you feel you are being obedient to God's calling and a tragedy occurs, how do you meet this challenge when tempted to comply no longer?

4. Why is it important for Christians to maintain their

faith and testimony when tragedy strikes?

5. What are some examples of Elijah's humility that you find illustrated in the 102 classroom?

6. When have you personally experienced great faith, and what was the outcome?

7. What are you thinking about in your plans that require great faith?

CLASS 201
Fire at Mt. Carmel

(Examination Time)

"Now it happened [after] many days that the word of the LORD came to Elijah in the third year, saying, 'Go, show yourself to Ahab, and I will send rain on the face of the earth.' So Elijah went to show himself to Ahab. Now the famine [was] severe in Samaria. Ahab called Obadiah who [was] over the household. (Now Obadiah feared the LORD greatly; for when Jezebel destroyed the prophets of the LORD, Obadiah took a hundred prophets and hid them by fifties in a cave, and provided them with bread and water.) Then Ahab said to Obadiah, 'Go through the land to all the springs of water and to all the valleys; perhaps we will find grass and keep the horses and mules alive, and not have to kill some of the cattle.' So they divided the land between them to survey it; Ahab went one way by himself and Obadiah went another way

by himself. Now as Obadiah was on the way, behold, Elijah met him, and he recognized him and fell on his face and said, 'Is this you, Elijah my master?' He said to him, 'It is I. Go, say to your master, Behold, Elijah [is here].' He said, 'What sin have I committed, that you are giving your servant into the hand of Ahab to put me to death? As the LORD your God lives, there is no nation or kingdom where my master has not sent to search for you; and when they said, He is not [here,] he made the kingdom or nation swear that they could not find you. And now you are saying, Go, say to your master, Behold, Elijah [is here.] It will come about when I leave you that the Spirit of the LORD will carry you where I do not know; so when I come and tell Ahab and he cannot find you, he will kill me, although [I] your servant have feared the LORD from my youth. Has it not been told to my master what I did when Jezebel killed the prophets of the LORD, that I hid a hundred prophets of the LORD by fifties in a cave, and provided them with bread and water? And now you are saying, Go, say to your master, Behold, Elijah [is here]; he will then kill me.' Elijah said, As the LORD of hosts lives, before whom I stand, I will surely show myself to him today.' So Obadiah went to meet Ahab and told him; and

Ahab went to meet Elijah. When Ahab saw Elijah, Ahab said to him, 'Is this you, you troubler of Israel?' He said, 'I have not troubled Israel, but you and your father's house [have], because you have forsaken the commandments of the LORD and you have followed the Baals. Now then send [and] gather to me all Israel at Mount Carmel, [together] with 450 prophets of Baal and 400 prophets of the Asherah, who eat at Jezebel's table.' So Ahab sent [a message] among all the sons of Israel and brought the prophets together at Mount Carmel. Elijah came near to all the people and said, 'How long [will] you hesitate between two opinions? If the LORD is God, follow Him; but if Baal, follow him.' But the people did not answer him a word. Then Elijah said to the people, 'I alone am left a prophet of the LORD, but Baal's prophets are 450 men. Now let them give us two oxen; and let them choose one ox for themselves and cut it up, and place it on the wood, but put no fire [under it]; and I will prepare the other ox and lay it on the wood, and I will not put a fire [under it]. Then you call on the name of your god, and I will call on the name of the LORD, and the God who answers by fire, He is God.' And all the people said, 'That is a good idea.' So Elijah said to the prophets of Baal, 'Choose one *ox for yourselves and prepare it first for you are many, and call on the name of your god, but put no fire [under it].' Then they took the ox which was given them and they prepared it and called on the name of Baal from morning until noon saying, O Baal, answer us. But there was no voice and no one answered. And they leaped about the altar which they made. It came about at noon, that Elijah mocked them and said, 'Call out with a loud voice, for he is a god; either he is occupied or gone aside, or is on a journey, or perhaps he is asleep and needs to be awakened.' So they cried with a loud voice and cut themselves according to their custom with swords and lances until the blood gushed out on them. When midday was past, they raved until the time of the offering of the [evening] sacrifice; but there was no voice, no one answered, and no one paid attention. Then Elijah said to all the people, 'Come near to me.' So all the people came near to him. And he repaired the altar of the LORD which had been torn down. Elijah took twelve stones according to the number of the tribes of the sons of Jacob, to whom the word of the LORD had come, saying, 'Israel shall be your name.' So with the stones he built an altar in the name of the LORD, and he made a trench around the altar, large enough to hold two measures of seed. Then he arranged the wood and cut the ox in pieces and laid [it] on the wood. And he said, 'Fill four pitchers with water and pour [it] on the burnt offering and on the wood.' And he said, 'Do it a second time,' and they did it a second time. And he said, 'Do it a third time,' and they did it a third time. The water flowed around the altar and he also filled the trench with water. At the time of the offering of the [evening] sacrifice, Elijah the prophet came near and said, 'O LORD, the God of Abraham, Isaac and Israel, to-day let it be known that You are God in Israel and that I am Your servant and I have done all these things at Your word. Answer me, O LORD, answer me, that this people may know that You, O LORD, are God, and [that] You have turned their heart back again.' Then the fire of the LORD fell and consumed the burnt offering and the wood and the stones and the dust, and licked up the water that was in the trench. When all the people saw it, they fell on their faces; and they said, 'The LORD, He is God; the LORD, He is God.' Then Elijah said to them, 'Seize the prophets of Baal; do not let one of them escape.' So they seized them; and Elijah brought them down to the brook Kishon, and slew them there. Now Elijah said to Ahab,*

'Go up, eat and drink; for there is the sound of the roar of a [heavy] shower.' So Ahab went up to eat and drink. But Elijah went up to the top of Carmel; and he crouched down on the earth and put his face between his knees. He said to his servant, 'Go up now, look toward the sea.' So he went up and looked and said, 'There is nothing.' And he said, 'Go back' seven times. It came about at the seventh [time], that he said, 'Behold, a cloud as small as a man's hand is coming up from the sea.' And he said, 'Go up, say to Ahab, Prepare [your chariot] and go down, so that the [heavy] shower does not stop you.' In a little while the sky grew black with clouds and wind, and there was a heavy shower. And Ahab rode and went to Jezreel. Then the hand of the LORD was on Elijah, and he girded up his loins and outran Ahab to Jezreel (1 Kings 18:1–46).

The objective in this class is to ascertain the level of comfort in displaying our faith publicly.

In the Mt. Carmel classroom, Elijah was given a significant test. Previously, God had sent him away from his comfort zone in Cherith and then into the dangerous arena of Zarephath. Until this point, Elijah had taken the following faith steps: At Cherith, only Elijah saw that God was faithful and powerful, but at Zarephath, Elijah, the widow, and her son saw God was faithful and powerful.

At Mt. Carmel, others would learn the above lessons. An essential component in a believer's maturation process will always involve situations where we see the same.

In his first two classrooms, Elijah saw God at work in private settings. Now, he would see God work publicly. Elijah was neither surprised nor hesitant when God moved him in this direction and to his next assignment. Elijah had learned his two previous lessons well and was now ready for his next classroom lesson.

After many days, God ordered Elijah to return to King Ahab: "The word of the LORD came to Elijah in the third year [of the drought], saying, 'Go, show yourself to Ahab, and I will send rain on the face of the earth'" (1 Kings 18:1).

Elijah set off to see the king. "So Elijah went to show himself to Ahab (1 Kings 18:2a). But his journey was not easily accomplished. Elijah carried the good news that rain would come soon. But the desperately needed rain had not come yet. The deadly drought continued. "[T]he famine was severe in Samaria" (1 Kings 18:2b). Elijah would not be a welcome visitor.

For Elijah to safely return to King Ahab's presence, he needed a protective escort. He needed someone who would not "shoot first and ask questions later." That person was Obadiah, a faithful servant of God who had proven his merit by providing food to one hundred of God's prophets. William A. Vangemeren wrote, "Elijah was God's first covenant prosecutor, for he charged Israel with its failure to conform to the covenantal expectations."[3] When believers proclaim a message of judgment that is unpopular and then see it executed, they require protection.

After Elijah and King Ahab met, the king attempted to use the prophet to his advantage. "When Ahab saw Elijah, Ahab said to him, 'Is this you, you troubler of Israel'" (1 Kings 18:17)? The king tried to place all blame for the deadly drought on Elijah. This is not an uncommon strategy used by our spiritual enemy. When unbelievers receive God's judgment and wrath, they quickly try to absolve themselves of personal guilt or responsibility. True offenders will seek out someone else to be a scapegoat, and the scapegoats today are often Christians.

But Elijah does not back down. He makes it quite clear that the king and his household were at fault and responsible for God's judgment: "[Elijah] said, 'I have not troubled Israel, but you and your father's House have, because you have forsaken the commandments of the LORD and you have followed the Baals'" (1 Kings 18:18). They needed to repent and take responsibility. Elijah also describes the king's sin. He had forsaken Yahweh's commands and had followed false gods.

Elijah then directly challenged the king. "Now then send and gather to me all Israel at Mount Carmel, together with 450 prophets of Baal and 400 prophets of the Asherah, who eat at Jezebel's table" (1 Kings 18:19). Elijah demanded a contest between His God and the false prophets of Baal. He no longer relied on mere words to prosecute the king and prove his guilt. As before — when Elijah summoned God's power to revive the dead son — he intended to ask for a miracle. Elijah wants God to demonstrate beyond all doubt that the king is guilty.

Until now, Elijah had been protected by God, encouraged in his actions, faithful in his obedience, and not intimidated by unbelievers — honorable characteristics for any believer.

In the competition, Elijah demands two oxen be slain and placed on an altar constructed of stone with wood on top. But no one was to set the food on fire. The prophets of Baal, numbering 450, would call on their god to light the fire. Elijah would likewise call on his God to do the same. The people agreed.

Elijah intended to demonstrate that Israel's God was the one true God. However, as the event unfolded, Elijah demanded that the people choose his God or Baal. "[H]ow long will you hesitate between two opinions? If the LORD is God, follow Him; but if Baal, follow him" (1 Kings 18:21).

Presently, Elijah did not direct his statements to King Ahab or the false prophets of Baal and Asherah. He was not asking them to choose between Baal or the God of Israel. They had already made their decision by rejecting God. Instead, Elijah ignored them and gave their opinions no weight, dignity, or credibility. There comes a time when we should no longer respectfully listen to the word of unbelievers, and that is what Elijah did.

Jesus said in Matthew 7:6, "Do not give what is holy to dogs, and do not throw your pearls before swine, or they will trample them under their feet, and turn and tear you to pieces."

Elijah pursued the lost sheep of Israel, trying desperately to persuade them to repent and return to the Lord. He was not concerned with those who had rejected Yahweh.

The people do not answer Elijah at that particular time. When an invitation to accept the Lord is given, people may not immediately respond positively or in any manner at all. In his Word Biblical Commentary, Simon J. DeVries states the following:

The Israelite people had been so confused by countering claims that they had been unable to decide. "The people answered not a word." They would not answer Elijah because they could not answer. Yahweh was their ancestral God, but the naturalistic appeal of the vegetative Baal religion had confused them.[4]

But Elijah was not disheartened or frustrated by the peoples' refusal to respond. Instead, he continued to pursue a decision. As long he did not receive a negative response, Elijah believed he was still required to proceed.

God answered Elijah's prayer and sent a fire that consumed the sacrifice, wood, stones, dust, and the water Elijah had poured over the sacrifice. The priests of Baal were exposed as false prophets, and Baal was shown to be a sham. It takes a supernatural act of God to convince the people that our holy God is the one and only God.

No one can come to the Lord and decide to follow Him unless God first reveals Himself and calls that person. We should appreciate that sacrifice after accepting it, but the Spirit must light the fire in our hearts and lead us to God.

After God supernaturally proved His sovereignty to the people, Elijah did something amazing and powerful. "Then Elijah said to them, 'Seize the prophets of Baal; do not let one of them escape.' So they seized them; and Elijah brought them down to the brook Kishon, and slew them there (1 Kings 18:40).

When God moves into our lives, we have no room for falsehood or lies. Elijah had to remove all evil influences so they could no longer contaminate God's people. We cannot provide a platform or medium from which evil can influence us and possibly others. We must directly confront evil. The psalmist said, "Hate evil, you who love the LORD (Psalm 97:10). Evil must be attacked and eradicated, not overlooked or ignored.

Elijah made the proclamation, cast the challenge, displayed God's power, and destroyed the enemy. The people respond by recognizing Israel's God as sovereign. "When all the people saw it, they fell on their faces; and they said, 'The LORD, He is God; the LORD, He is God'" (1 Kings 18:39).

But Elijah could not relax and rejoice in the victorious fruits of his labor. Work remained, and more lessons had to be learned by Elijah in the Mt. Carmel classroom.

Next, Elijah responded to God's promise of rain. Three years and six months had passed since rain had fallen. It would not be surprising for Elijah to entertain doubts once again. Surely, he received negative responses, claiming that no rain would fall. Satan is undoubtedly angry that Baal and the Asherah priests were exposed as frauds. Now, he wanted revenge.

However, by this time, Elijah had developed a strong confidence in the Lord's faithfulness. Elijah had come to trust in the Lord. He had experienced God's loyalty and comfort a long time before in Cherith. At Cherith, Elijah had taken time to study creation and see God's handiwork in the stars, vegetation, etc. Elijah recognized the faithfulness God displayed by providing water and food.

Later, Elijah was protected while in Zarephath, Queen Jezebel's homeland. After those experiences, Elijah's faith grew and strengthened. How could Elijah ever doubt that God would provide the needed rain? Neither should we doubt God's promises. We should recall what we have witnessed regarding God's faithfulness. He has been and will always be faithful to us. This knowledge provides an excellent weapon with which to defeat Satan's assaults.

In this classroom, we also learn persistence. In 1 Kings 18:43, we read that Elijah's servant goes out seven times to scan the sky for rain clouds. Finally, he saw "a cloud as small as man's hand" in the sky. Elijah knew God had answered his prayer. The desired rain came slowly and subtly. Elijah recognized the decisive significance of the rain. When God promises to do something, we should confidently expect its occurrence. We must be patient and persevere, even if we have to seek God's work repeatedly as Elijah did. Recall the prayer Moses made in Exodus 33:18: "I pray You, show me Your glory!"

Elijah's concern for King Ahab before any rain fell was of slightly lesser but still significant importance. Although the cloud was small, Elijah knew a rainstorm would end the long drought. So Elijah sent word to the king, telling him to seek shelter. "Prepare your chariot and go down, so that the heavy shower does not stop you" (1 Kings 18:44).

Why would Elijah warn the same evil king whom he had recently condemned? We would think the king's safety would be the last thing on Elijah's mind. Yet, Elijah knew the king's safety was necessary at the moment. This exemplifies Christian love in action.

Insights for Reflection

Students in a university are typically given their exams at two time periods: the midterm and the end. This means students face multiple exams on various subjects within a brief period. As a result, they have no time to rest or relax.

One of Elijah's tests was whether he could pursue

his commitment to the Lord. Before Elijah went to King Ahab and then on to Mt. Carmel, he conversed with Obadiah, who feared King Ahab would kill him if he followed Elijah's directions. Obadiah accused Elijah of putting him in harm's way if Elijah continued to yield to God's Spirit.

Believers are often warned that their devotion to God's calling might bring personal harm or trouble to their families. We must guard against such impudence as we follow Christ.

Elijah had to confront two idol gods, Baal and Asherah, as well as the many false prophets who proclaimed and promoted those false gods. Baal and Asherah represented fertility for crops and for procreation, while Asherah represented sensuality. While such desires in their proper use are not sinful, they are often wrongfully pursued outside God's plan.

The believer encounters these same gods, but not in the same form. Any attempt to obtain wealth, power, and sexual pleasure independent of God's prescribed ways is idolatry. We are wise to avoid these sinful gods and the people who worship and promote them.

Elijah may have experienced anxiety when his servant continually reported an absence of rain clouds, but Elijah never doubted God's promise. We, too, may waver if we do not receive an immediate answer to our prayers. But Elijah trusted and persisted. By this time, Elijah's faith had matured to a higher level. He knew God's timetable was not always ours, yet one we could depend on. All upper-level students should have learned this same lesson.

Few students enjoy tests. They are stressful and rarely enjoyable, but they are necessary to determine whether a student has learned the lesson. God can use fire to strengthen a believer's faith. The fire on Mt. Carmel helped those under Obadiah's care to strengthen their faith.

I experienced a unique event where fire impacted me. Early one morning, around one a.m., I received a call from my plant manager, requesting I come quickly to our factory, which was on fire. After arriving, I saw seven fire trucks fighting to extinguish major flames throughout our company's buildings. Standing in shock, all I could do was wonder, "Why God?"

Fonzie, the plant manager, put his arm around me and said, "Let's pray."

I said, "Fonzie, I don't feel like praying right now because my faith is not strong."

Fonzie replied, "Ed, rest on my faith for now."

This event indicated where I was spiritually and that I needed Christian support in times of adversity. God can use our struggles as teaching moments in some of the most challenging circumstances, even when we don't expect or think it necessary. As God provided Obadiah for Elijah, He provided Fonzie for me. With Fonzie's help, I rebuilt my company and had an even greater factory.

Students begrudgingly accept that they will undergo examinations and that their knowledge will be tested. But such testing does not always occur in the manner the student expects. Such testing is prepared and brought forth by the teacher, not by the student. It is the teacher who determines the time of the testing as well as its subject matter. The teacher decides how to display the student's knowledge (multiple choice, essay, etc.) Also, the teacher determines whether the student's answers and interpretations are correct.

We are not always privy to God's timetable when scheduling our examinations. God may test each of us at any time and in any way. How long such testing occurs and the reason for such divine examinations might confuse us, but we must remain firm in our faith and trust that God's wisdom is greater. We must face each test with humble faith, believing God is out for our betterment.

Questions

1. When a fellow believer fears obeying God's instruction in the face of danger, how can you help?

2. How can you overcome your fears when God calls you to action, but you are in a potentially dangerous situation?

3. Elijah had to display his faith in a public setting openly. Would this be a problem for you? Why or why not?

4. Ahab accused Elijah of being the cause of the drought. Does the world blame Christians for human suffering today? What defense can you provide when confronted with such accusations?

5. What is a good definition of a miracle that aligns with the biblical conception?

6. Can you elaborate on an occasion when you felt the need to display your faith in a public setting?

CLASS 202
Mt. Horeb

(Depression)

"Now Ahab told Jezebel all that Elijah had done, and how he had killed all the prophets with the sword. Then Jezebel sent a messenger to Elijah, saying, 'So may the gods do to me and even more, if I do not make your life as the life of one of them by tomorrow about this time.' And he was afraid and arose and ran for his life and came to Beersheba, which belongs to Judah, and left his servant there. But he himself went a day's journey into the wilderness, and came and sat down under a juniper tree; and he requested for himself that he might die, and said, 'It is enough; now, O LORD, take my life, for I am not better than my fathers.' He lay down and slept under a juniper tree; and behold, there was an angel touching him, and he said to him, 'Arise, eat.' Then he looked and behold, there was at his head a bread cake [baked on] hot stones,

and a jar of water. So he ate and drank and lay down again. The angel of the LORD came again a second time and touched him and said, 'Arise, eat, because the journey is too great for you.' So he arose and ate and drank, and went in the strength of that food forty days and forty nights to Horeb, the mountain of God. Then he came there to a cave and lodged there; and behold, the word of the LORD [came] to him, and He said to him, 'What are you doing here, Elijah?' He said, 'I have been very zealous for the LORD, the God of hosts; for the sons of Israel have forsaken Your covenant, torn down Your altars and killed Your prophets with the sword. And I alone am left; and they seek my life, to take it away.' So He said, 'Go forth and stand on the mountain before the LORD.' And behold, the LORD was passing by! And a great and strong wind was rending the mountains and breaking in pieces the rocks before the LORD; [but] the LORD [was] not in the wind. And after the wind an earthquake, [but] the LORD [was] not in the earthquake. After the earthquake a fire, [but] the LORD [was] not in the fire; and after the fire a sound of a gentle blowing. When Elijah heard [it], he wrapped his face in his mantle and went out and stood in the entrance of the cave. And behold, a voice [came] to him and said, 'What are you doing here, Elijah?' Then he said, 'I have been very zealous for the LORD, the God of hosts; for the sons of Israel have forsaken Your covenant, torn down your altars and killed Your prophets with the sword. And I alone am left; and they seek my life, to take it away.' The LORD said to him, 'Go, return on your way to the wilderness of Damascus, and when you have arrived, you shall anoint Hazael king over Aram; and Jehu the son of Nimshi you shall anoint king over Israel; and Elisha the son of Shaphat of Abel-meholah you shall anoint as prophet in your place. It shall come about, the one who escapes from the sword of Hazael, Jehu shall put to death, and the one who escapes from the sword of Jehu, Elisha shall put to death. Yet I will leave 7,000 in Israel, all the knees that have not bowed to Baal and every mouth that has not kissed him.' So he departed from there and found Elisha the son of Shaphat, while he was plowing with twelve pairs [of oxen] before him, and he with the twelfth. And Elijah passed over to him and threw his mantle on him. He left the oxen and ran after Elijah and said, 'Please let me kiss my father and my mother, then I will follow you.' And he said to him, 'Go back again, for what have I done to you?' So he returned from following *him, and took the pair of oxen and sacrificed them and boiled their flesh with the implements of the oxen, and gave [it] to the people and they ate. Then he arose and followed Elijah and ministered to him (1 Kings 19:1–21).*

The objective of this class is to teach us to share our true spiritual feelings honestly with God.

Elijah and his God were victorious. Elijah had boldly approached King Ahab and courageously outlined the king's guilt. He had taken on Baal and his prophets in a contest to the death and prevailed. He had patiently waited for the word of God to be fulfilled, and God rewarded his patience and prayers. Finally, the promised rain came just as God had promised.

But Elijah's success was not acclaimed by everyone. Heeding the advice given by Elijah, King Ahab traveled to Jezreel, the home of his wife, Queen Jezebel. The king told the queen all that Elijah had accomplished, including how he had killed the false prophets. To put it mildly, the queen was not pleased. She wanted revenge. She wanted Elijah to die quickly. So, she sent her threat to Elijah: "So may the gods do to me and even more, if I do not make your life as the life of one of them by tomorrow about this time" (1 Kings 19:2).

Elijah took the queen's threat seriously. He ran for his life, traveling some 120 miles to the town of Beersheba in the kingdom of Judah. There, Elijah left his servant and went further into the wilderness. He sat under a juniper tree and asked God to let him die. "It is enough; now O LORD, take my life, for I am not better than my fathers (1 Kings 19:4).

By reviewing Scripture, we can determine that Elijah's education in the Mt. Horeb classroom occurred at two separate locations: an alcove in Beersheba and Mt. Horeb. The alcove was where Elijah had run when the Scriptures said he fled for his life to Beersheba — a place rich in Old Testament history.

We might ask why Elijah ran. Why was he so afraid? Why would a man who had been so successful for God panic and flee? Why would the queen's threat frighten him so? And then, after reaching a haven far from the queen, why did he pray to die?

As strange as it may appear, such behavior is not uncommon. We read of a similar emotional experience in Jonah 4:3. After Jonah had finally obeyed God's command and preached a successful message to pagans in Nineveh, he became severely depressed. The Scriptures also include several testimonies of depression from such godly men as Moses (Numbers 11:15) and Job (Job 10:18–21, Job 6:8–9, Job 3:11). David in Psalm 55:6–8, Paul in 2 Corinthians 1:8, and many others have also given voice to melancholy statements of bitter despair. Those men also reached a point of anguish where the effort to continue seemed beyond their ability. So, Elijah was in good company.

Still, we wonder what caused the deep depression experienced by this faithful man of God. One possible answer involves Elijah's expectation of human help. Elijah may have been discouraged and saddened because no one came to his defense when Queen Jezebel pronounced her public death decree. After all, had Elijah not demonstrated the incredible power and majesty of the One True God? Why then did believing supporters not come forward to defend and protect him? Why did no one provide sanctuary for him? We see evidence that such questions may have been in Elijah's mind when he later told God he was the only true believer left. "I alone am left; and they seek my life, to take it away" (1 King 19:10).

Elijah's depression could also have been a cumulative effect of physical and emotional exhaustion. He had been under tremendous pressure for a long time. He had not had any conventional full-course meals. With the limited diet at Cherith and the unlimited menu at Zarephath, his body might have been depleted of needed nutrients. Add to this that he had just completed a long foot race against a team of Ahab's chariot horses and then traveled over a hundred miles in a fearful panic. He probably had not slept in several days. The total effect was that he was physically exhausted.

Emotionally, Elijah had been accused of treason, causing sorrow, and unreliability. Now, he had a death threat on him. The classroom of Beersheba, although an alcove, was required to teach him there is a time when everyone needs to get away for rest. Elijah was no doubt also spiritually exhausted. He struggled to understand God's ways in the many unexpected and difficult predicaments he had endured.

Elijah's first reaction when entering the Beersheba classroom was to lie down and ask God to take his life — and he believed God would. God responded to

Elijah's prayer but not in the fashion Elijah expected. Instead, God did the opposite by refreshing Elijah. God sent an angel to give him food and water. After Elijah rested, the angel returned to feed him again. The angel said, "Arise, eat, because the journey is too great for you" (1 Kings 19:7). The food had such nutritional strength that Elijah survived for forty days and nights as he traveled to Mt. Horeb (1 Kings 19:8). Many times, when we also feel the overpowering weight of despair, God will lead us to rest and then strengthen us for the work ahead.

Also interesting is that the angel of the LORD prepared Elijah's meal (1 Kings 19:7). Although we cannot be sure, most references to this angel imply deity, making it possible that this angel was God Himself in the person of Christ. The use of that particular phrase suggests that it is in fact God Himself in the person of His Son (Jesus, the Messiah) who has come to personally minister to the welfare of His beloved servant Elijah. Such conjecture has strong merit, as God has consistently demonstrated His love and care for His children. A strong argument can be made that it is Jesus Himself, in a pre-incarnate appearance, ministering to Elijah.

Also, in Exodus 34:6 we read God's own words in which He describes Himself as compassionate and gracious, slow to anger and abounding in loving kindness and truth. These are God's words and not those of an angel or patriarch or priest or prophet. (It is a possibility, but not a certainty, and not a battleground issue.)

The Beersheba classroom taught Elijah and us more about God's response of loving grace to our human frailty. We see how God might respond to our pitiable prayers, physiological needs, and emotional distress. The Lord never rebuked Elijah, nor did He pressure him. Instead, He gave Elijah the food, drink, rest, and time he needed to regain his strength and continue his divine mission.

But we must leave the alcove and enter the Mt. Horeb classroom. God favored this location, and it was the first area where God called Moses. We could call Mt. Horeb "God's neighborhood" because Moses spent forty days and nights here alone with God. It is also the place where God first gave the Law.

Elijah had heard God speak at Thisbe, Samaria, Cherith, and Zarephath. However, it was only at Mt. Horeb that God fully revealed Himself to Elijah in a unique and overpowering manner.

Elijah traveled alone from Beersheba to Mt. Horeb, but he was not alone. God traveled with him. Elijah was impervious to the route's dangers since he was undoubtedly driven onward by God's Spirit. F. W. Krummacher observed that during this journey, Elijah probably reflected on the Mosaic journey in the wilderness and the remarkable experiences the people of Israel encountered at that time.[5]

As part of our training, God often leads us into meditative moments where we can reflect on our Christian heritage. We are not the first to experience such trials and difficulties. Knowing others overcame their sufferings and obstacles with God's help can encourage us.

When Elijah arrived at Mt. Horeb, he was exhausted, tired, and spent. The effects of the supernatural food had probably worn off. Additionally, he may have felt a sense of complete and total loneliness. Perhaps, he entered the cave as protection from predators — or to hide. Some theologians think the cave or cleft may have been the same cleft in which God placed Moses when He revealed His full glory (Exodus 33:21–22).

The sun may have been setting when Elijah arrived. As he lay down, he probably entertained thoughts and fears about his situation. Then, he heard God's voice: "What are you doing here, Elijah?" (1 Kings 19:9). Of course, God was not asking Elijah a real question. He knew why Elijah was there. God wanted Elijah to voice his thoughts. Elijah then complains to God that all of Israel has turned away from God. The "sons of Israel" have killed all of God's prophets. Elijah alone is left alive. He is the only one remaining who remains "very zealous for the LORD." And after all that, Elijah tells God that now the people are trying to kill him too: "[T]hey seek my life, to take it away."

We might expect God to answer Elijah's list of grievances that he was unworthy to continue his godly work and that no one was left who cared about God. But, instead, Elijah felt he could not continue.

Although God will eventually address Elijah's lament, He first arranges a demonstration for His loyal servant — one necessary for Elijah to understand that God will not always manifest Himself as we expect. Elijah needed to learn outward appearances are not necessarily an indication of God's presence. God told Elijah,

"Go forth and stand on the mountain before the LORD." A strong wind arose, breaking the mountains into pieces. Then, an earthquake occurred, followed by fire and the "sound of a gentle blowing" (1 Kings 19:11–12).

God uses three of nature's elements at Mt. Horeb: wind, earthquakes, and fire. These are examples of tremendous raw natural power. The Scriptures record that God uses elements of nature as tools to chasten His people. Isaiah 29:6 records God using the earthquake, whirlwind, tempest, and fire to discipline His people. God may even manifest Himself amid such elements, as when He allowed Isaiah and Ezekiel to see His glory (Isaiah 6, Ezekiel 1).

But why and by what method God chooses to display His power is for God to decide. We become myopic when we think, as Elijah did, that things are not going well because they do not appear as Christ-confirming. God is never limited to methodology, manifestation, discipline, or communication. He must, however, abide within His standard of holiness, righteousness, and divinity.

Only after His tremendous demonstration of ferocious physical strength did God manifest Himself at the opposite end of the power spectrum. God's voice was low and soft, like a gentle whisper. Why? God wanted to draw Elijah close to Him. "Come closer to Me," we can almost hear God calling out to Elijah. "Come into My presence." Such compassionate warmth and peace after a powerful display of energetic climactic forces would have amazed and puzzled Elijah. A classroom that teaches such extremes about God and His power is a successful classroom. We cannot box God into a set standard constructed by human ingenuity.

God asked Elijah a second time why he was in the cave (1 Kings 19:13). Again, Elijah complained about his bleak situation. On the second occasion, God answered Elijah and sent him to Damascus with full instructions to pursue a new mission. God also informed Elijah that a new prophet, Elisha, would take his place. Additionally, God told Elijah he was not alone. Another seven thousand believers in Israel had "not bowed to Baal" (1 Kings 19:18).

God's response was one Elijah could easily comprehend. Like Elijah, we may have many questions for God concerning our beliefs about Him or complaints against Him. But until we develop a greater understanding of

God's power and attributes, we will never comprehend, much less accept, His rulings and direction for our lives.

Now that Elijah had learned others were not ignoring his ministry and that he was not ineffective, he was ready for God's next assignment. The Lord had addressed Elijah's physical, emotional, and theological needs. Then, He addressed Elijah's anticipation and curiosity. As Elijah prepared to leave Mt. Horeb's classroom and go on to the next one, he wondered what would happen to the people of Israel and him. His main concern would be his replacement.

Let us follow Elijah to his next learning arena: the Naboth vineyard.

Insights for Reflection

College life can be both exhilarating and disappointing. Suicide ranks among the leading causes of death for college students. But why? This should be the age when young people enjoy the happiest and most carefree time of their lives. After all, they usually carry minimal responsibility to others and enjoy optimal physical health. They feel they have the answers to all life's questions and see a bright and joyous future. When

I was a junior in college, I thought I could improve the world with my suggestions — if only I could get people to listen to me.

But God does not promise us a life filled only with happiness, pleasure, and joy. I learned that lesson the hard way. I have experienced personal tragedies such as leukemia, coronary artery failure, business setbacks, family disturbances, and demolished dreams that initially seemed unfair. What good purpose did they serve? But each strengthened my faith in God and reliance on the greatest teacher, Jesus Christ.

When accepted reverently and viewed as opportunities for spiritual growth, life's disappointments compose a necessary element in God's curriculum and our sanctification process. Therefore, a student should accept them as a secondary step in salvation after justification but before glorification.

Disappointments seem to occur most unexpectedly and often after a great spiritual victory. For me, this happened in the spring of 1999. I had driven my family to church on a beautiful morning. I had recently been honored as a deacon, chosen as chairman of a new Christian academy, and received an ovation for my

Christian testimony at a large business conference.

Suddenly, without warning, another car rammed our vehicle, flipping us over and slamming us into a nearby pole. My wife and I were seriously injured and spent many weeks recovering in separate hospitals after multiple operations. Thankfully, our children were not hurt. Days later, after I regained consciousness, I questioned why God would let that happen. After all, I lived a life dedicated to honoring Him as best as I could.

Depression worked its way into my soul, and it took many days of prayer, Bible reading, and reflection to understand and accept what God was doing. In time, I gained a greater understanding of God, and not just in an academic or intellectual sense. God is always in control. He does not base His love for us on our merit, nor does it change with our circumstances. The accident was necessary for my spiritual growth.

Elijah has proven to be a true and faithful prophet, but he did not see the great revival he expected. Where was the massive conversion he probably expected? When we successfully carry out God's assignment, we often want to see immediate and positive results. When we do not, we tend to grow discouraged. When this happens, we must continue our work and remember God is still working. Only He decides when the work is complete.

The Bible says in Psalm 119:105, "Your word is a lamp to my feet and a light to my path." God does not always reveal the entire journey but typically only shows us the next step after we have completed the previous one. But not immediately recognizing any positive results and feeling emotional despair does not mean God has terminated our ministry.

Questions

1. Reflect on a time when you faced depression. How did you react, and how did you overcome it? What was the final resolution?

2. God used physical nourishment and rest to restore His prophet's mental health. God also gave him a new job assignment and a friend. Are these still good remedies for Christians today? Are there any additional treatments you can use to help a Christian suffering from depression?

3. Should depression always be viewed as a negative ailment?

4. Elijah took the threat from Jezebel seriously, caus-

ing him to flee. Is this a good practice to follow whenever someone threatens us? Why or why not?

5. Scripture mentions several forces of nature confronting Elijah before he heard God's voice. How does this show that God's ways of communication are not limited?

6. How can you discern when God is speaking and when He is not?

7. What did you feel about God and His plan when you experienced depression? What did you learn about God?

CLASS 301
The Vineyard

(Off-Campus Teaching)

"Now it came about after these things that Naboth the Jezreelite had a vineyard which [was] in Jezreel beside the palace of Ahab king of Samaria. Ahab spoke to Naboth, saying, 'Give me your vineyard, that I may have it for a vegetable garden because it is close beside my house, and I will give you a better vineyard than it in its place; if you like, I will give you the price of it in money.' But Naboth said to Ahab, 'The LORD forbid me that I should give you the inheritance of my fathers.' So Ahab came into his house sullen and vexed because of the word which Naboth the Jezreelite had spoken to him; for he said, 'I will not give you the inheritance of my fathers.' And he lay down on his bed and turned away his face and ate no food. But Jezebel his wife came to him and said to him, 'How is it that your spirit is so sullen

that you are not eating food?' So he said to her, 'Because I spoke to Naboth the Jezreelite and said to him, Give me your vineyard for money; or else, if it pleases you, I will give you a vineyard in its place. But he said, I will not give you my vineyard.' Jezebel his wife said to him, 'Do you now reign over Israel? Arise, eat bread, and let your heart be joyful; I will give you the vineyard of Naboth the Jezreelite.' So she wrote letters in Ahab's name and sealed them with his seal, and sent letters to the elders and to the nobles who were living with Naboth in his city. Now she wrote in the letters, saying, 'Proclaim a fast and seat Naboth at the head of the people; and seat two worthless men before him, and let them testify against him, saying, You cursed God and the king. Then take him out and stone him to death.' So the men of his city, the elders and the nobles who lived in his city, did as Jezebel had sent [word] to them, just as it was written in the letters which she had sent them. They proclaimed a fast and seated Naboth at the head of the people. Then the two worthless men came in and sat before him; and the worthless men testified against him, even against Naboth, before the people, saying, 'Naboth cursed God and the king.' So they took him outside the city and stoned him to death with stones. Then they sent [word] to Jezebel, saying, 'Naboth has been stoned and is dead.' When Jezebel heard that Naboth had been stoned and was dead, Jezebel said to Ahab, 'Arise, take possession of the vineyard of Naboth, the Jezreelite, which he refused to give you for money; for Naboth is not alive, but dead.' When Ahab heard that Naboth was dead, Ahab arose to go down to the vineyard of Naboth the Jezreelite, to take possession of it. Then the word of the LORD came to Elijah the Tishbite, saying, 'Arise, go down to meet Ahab king of Israel, who is in Samaria; behold, he is in the vineyard of Naboth where he has gone down to take possession of it. You shall speak to him, saying, Thus says the LORD, Have you murdered and also taken possession? And you shall speak to him, saying, Thus says the LORD, In the place where the dogs licked up the blood of Naboth the dogs will lick up your blood, even yours.' Ahab said to Elijah, 'Have you found me, O my enemy?' And he answered, 'I have found [you], because you have sold yourself to do evil in the sight of the LORD. Behold, I will bring evil upon you, and will utterly sweep you away, and will cut off from Ahab every male, both bond and free in Israel; and I will make your house like the house of Jeroboam the son of Nebat, and like the house of Baasha the son of Ahijah, because of the provocation with which you have provoked [Me] to anger, and [because] you have made Israel sin. Of Jezebel also has the LORD spoken, saying, The dogs will eat Jezebel in the district of Jezreel. The one belonging to Ahab, who dies in the city, the dogs will eat, and the one who dies in the field the birds of heaven will eat.' Surely there was no one like Ahab who sold himself to do evil in the sight of the LORD, because Jezebel his wife incited him. He acted very abominably in following idols, according to all that the Amorites had done, whom the LORD cast out before the sons of Israel. It came about when Ahab heard these words, that he tore his clothes and put on sackcloth and fasted, and he lay in sackcloth and went about despondently. Then the word of the LORD came to Elijah the Tishbite, saying, 'Do you see how Ahab has humbled himself before Me? Because he has humbled himself before Me, I will not bring the evil in his days, [but] I will bring the evil upon his house in his son's days'" (1 Kings 21:1–29).

The objective of this class is to ascertain one's willingness to remain obedient when placed in a dangerous environment.

A period of time had elapsed in Elijah's journeys between 1 Kings 19 and 21. By this time, King Ahab had successfully waged war and returned to his family's estate at Jezreel.

In summary, 1 Kings 21 tells us that a vineyard is located next to the estate owned by King Ahab. The vineyard is owned by a godly man named Naboth. King Ahab desires the vineyard for himself, so he offers to either purchase it from Naboth outright or exchange another piece of property of equal value for it. But Naboth refuses the king's offers, because to do so would violate the Mosaic Law regarding ancestral property sales. God has stated that all the Israelites' land is His and that it is never to be sold to anyone. (Leviticus 25:23)

King Ahab's wife, Queen Jezebel, has no respect at all for the Mosaic Law. She arranges for Naboth to be killed. King Ahab will then obtain the property by the law of kingship default.

Queen Jezebel's plan succeeds. Naboth is killed and

the vineyard comes under King Ahab's ownership. It is into that arena God now calls Elijah so that the prophet may pronounce judgment upon the king and his family for such a terribly atrocious act.

The narrative subjects were primarily Naboth, Queen Jezebel, and King Ahab. Elijah is mentioned only as an agent of God's righteous judgment. Nevertheless, this was still a classroom learning experience. Elijah recognized justice was applied equally to everyone, regardless of a person's rank or position in society. King Ahab received a severe sentence even though he was neither the author nor a direct participant in the crime.

The punishment was in direct proportion to the crime itself. As Naboth and his sons were executed, so would King Ahab and his sons experience the same. As dogs licked Naboth's blood, so too would dogs lick the blood of King Ahab and Queen Jezebel. As Naboth was not permitted to enjoy his vineyard, neither would King Ahab enjoy it. As Naboth's widow and children would lose their inheritance of the vineyard, so too would King Ahab's widow, Queen Jezebel, and his children lose the vineyard. Finally, as Naboth's reputation was soiled, so too would King Ahab lose his reputation.

Nevertheless, the mercy of God was fully displayed after Ahab, in the act of repentance, tore his clothes and fasted (1 Kings 21:29).

God continued to protect Elijah, even as he proclaimed judgment on an evil king. Elijah was in the company of King Ahab's servants, who could have easily killed him if ordered.

God continued to use Elijah with the gifts He had given him. But God never called Elijah to speak on national political issues. He was more concerned with the people's character than a nation's territories and dependencies. Instead, God used other prophets for those purposes.

As God had assigned a unique role to Elijah, He also has a special role and duty for us. This is illustrated in the New Testament when the Apostle Paul speaks of God distributing the gifts of the Spirit among church members in various ways (Ephesians 4).

We can learn the above lessons by observing others. By witnessing God's treatment of King Ahab, we can also receive further insight into God's divine character.

"Ahab," writes William Taylor, "was on the throne

of Israel with every comfort and luxury which wealth and rank could confer, yet hankering after more, and, when that was denied him, filled with the bitterest mortification."[6]

Regardless of how much wealth we possess, our sinful nature will move us to crave more. By nature, we are never satisfied with the offerings of this world.

Taylor further observed, "If at the moment of [King Ahab's] disappointment, he had been blessed with a godly wife, she would have led him to think of the comforts which he already possessed, and, far from setting herself to acquire for him the object of his desire by unlawful means, she would have urged him to seek his happiness in something nobler than the vineyard of his neighbor. As it was, Queen Jezebel only added the guilty sins of conspiracy and murder to that of covetousness."[7]

The progression of sin was not unique to this historical account. We see the same pattern as early as the fall of Adam and Eve. Any sin, if not checked, will continue its destructive course, eventually involving as many participants and victims as possible. Reverend Michael Lawrence has provided excellent comments on the progressive pattern of sin in his book Biblical

Theology in the Life of the Church. He stated: "What's more, the Fall is progressive, not static. Things didn't just go from good to bad. Rather, things continued to get worse. They don't stay the same, and they don't get better. It's like a fatal disease that begins at a point in time, but then progresses and runs its ever increasing destructive course."[8]

Queen Jezebel was well-acquainted with the Mosaic Law and its requirements but still violated it. It is not uncommon for people to pervert the Scriptures and use them to justify their sinful behavior. Although such an attempt is abhorrent, it is a tactic that the educated Christian should be aware of as we deal with society. Satan and his demons know the Bible well, but they will twist and misuse it to lead people astray. Likewise, people will also employ God's Word to give a righteous flavor to their sinful activities.

William Taylor once again provides an excellent commentary on this subject: "Your educated villains are all the more dangerous because of their education; and among godless men they are the most to be dreaded who have an intelligent acquaintance with the Word of God."[9]

In summary, the vineyard classroom teaches us about God's mercy and judgment. It also teaches us about the treacherous schemes of the sinner and the destructive powers of sin itself.

Insights for Reflection

One of the benefits many university students enjoy is the knowledge they gain from other students. We can learn a great deal from others, and they can help us grow and develop. They can also draw us back to the proper path should we go astray. Proverbs 27:17 states, "Iron sharpens iron, so one man sharpens another." Had King Ahab had an accountability partner to curb his covetous desire for another man's property, the king could have overcome that temptation.

Unfortunately, being a student at God's University does not automatically protect us from temptation nor free us from our duty to proclaim God's Word to others. Believers are always on duty and may be called on at any time to deliver a message to others.

I saw this principle illustrated through an event on a Navy warship. The Navy had invited me to be their guest aboard a nuclear aircraft carrier while conducting maneuvers at sea. Once I landed on deck, I was assigned to a junior naval officer who escorted me to my cabin and the various departments around the ship. During my stay, I was told that at certain times this officer would bring me to the bridge to meet the ship's captain. I would also meet the admiral of the fleet of supporting ships surrounding the carrier. The junior officer was excited. When I asked him why, he replied, "Edward, because of you, I now get to meet and have an audience with the most senior personnel. Please put in a good word for me and tell them how well I served you."

This illustrates how a Christian can be blessed to provide opportunities for others to meet our Captain, Jesus Christ. While this episode benefited the sailor, it also teaches about our responsibility to invite people to trust Jesus Christ as their Savior.

Serving as ambassadors for encouragement is joyful and rewarding. Like Elijah, however, God may have us advise people about His judgment on sin. This is never pleasant and can become a dangerous confrontation, as was the case with the prophet and King Ahab.

What can we learn from Elijah's participation in

this narrative? First, God called Elijah to confront an old adversary. We often feel that once we reach a certain maturity level in our faith, we should no longer have to deal with old enemies or former trials.

Second, King Ahab still viewed Elijah as an enemy even though his kingdom once again enjoyed plentiful agricultural riches and abundance that God had given in response to Elijah's prayers. We should pray for our enemies as instructed by Jesus, but we should not think we will always gain favor with our adversaries.

Third, Elijah did not become angry at God when God withheld judgment on King Ahab because he repented. Elijah's attitude contrasted with Jonah's hatred for the pagans living in Ninevah (Jonah 3:10, 4:1–11).

Fourth, God tutored Elijah on how humility can appeal to God and affect God dispensing justice. King Ahab, hearing of God's pronouncement of justice, humbled himself before the Lord: "It came about when Ahab heard these words, that he tore his clothes and put on sackcloth and fasted, and he lay in sackcloth and went about despondently" (1 Kings 21:27). That act of submissiveness delayed God's punishment.

Questions

1. God called Elijah to return to a dangerous environment and confront his old enemies with a judicial judgment. As Christians, how can we muster the courage to fulfill a similar task when called to do likewise?

2. Ahab did not see his sin against Naboth. Why do you think it is easier for an individual to see sin in others but not recognize their own sins?

3. How have you dealt with strong sinful temptations that confront you?

4. God bestowed mercy on Ahab after he humbled himself before God. What does this tell you about the nature of God?

CLASS 302
The Hill

(Reflections of College)

"Now Moab rebelled against Israel after the death of Ahab. And Ahaziah fell through the lattice in his upper chamber which [was] in Samaria, and became ill. So he sent messengers and said to them, 'Go, inquire of Baal-zebub, the god of Ekron, whether I will recover from this sickness.' But the angel of the LORD said to Elijah the Tishbite, 'Arise, go up to meet the messengers of the king of Samaria and say to them, Is it because there is no God in Israel [that] you are going to inquire of Baal-zebub, the god of Ekron? Now therefore thus says the LORD, You shall not come down from the bed where you have gone up, but you shall surely die.' Then Elijah departed. When the messengers returned to him he said to them, 'Why have you returned?' They said to him, 'A man came up to meet us and said to us, Go, return to the king who sent

you and say to him, Thus says the LORD, Is it because there is no God in Israel [that] you are sending to inquire of Baal-zebub, the god of Ekron? Therefore you shall not come down from the bed where you have gone up, but shall surely die.' He said to them, 'What kind of man was he who came up to meet you and spoke these words to you?' They answered him, '[He was] a hairy man with a leather girdle bound about his loins.' And he said, 'It is Elijah the Tishbite.' Then [the king] sent to him a captain of fifty with his fifty. And he went up to him, and behold, he was sitting on the top of the hill. And he said to him, 'O man of God, the king says, Come down.' Elijah replied to the captain of fifty, 'If I am a man of God, let fire come down from heaven and consume you and your fifty.' Then fire came down from heaven and consumed him and his fifty. So he again sent to him another captain of fifty with his fifty. And he said to him, 'O man of God, thus says the king, Come down quickly.' Elijah replied to them, 'If I am a man of God, let fire come down from heaven and consume you and your fifty.' Then the fire of God came down from heaven and consumed him and his fifty. So he again sent the captain of a third fifty with his fifty. When the third captain of fifty went up, he came and bowed down on his knees before Elijah, and begged him and said to him, 'O man of God, please let my life and the lives of these fifty servants of yours be precious in your sight. Behold fire came down from heaven and consumed the first two captains of fifty with their fifties; but now let my life be precious in your sight.' The angel of the LORD said to Elijah, 'Go down with him; do not be afraid of him.' So he arose and went down with him to the king. Then he said to him, 'Thus says the LORD, Because you have sent messengers to inquire of Baal-zebub, the god of Ekron is it because there is no God in Israel to inquire of His word? Therefore you shall not come down from the bed where you have gone up, but shall surely die.' So Ahaziah died according to the word of the LORD which Elijah had spoken. And because he had no son, Jehoram became king in his place in the second year of Jehoram the son of Jehoshaphat, king of Judah. Now the rest of the acts of Ahaziah which he did, are they not written in the Book of the Chronicles of the Kings of Israel?" (2 Kings 1:1–18).

The objective of this class is to ascertain how effectively we hear and understand God's voice.

Elijah was now far along in his academic studies. He had seen God meet his physiological, social, and mental needs. He had witnessed God's power in both public and private settings. God had revealed Himself to Elijah in both orthodox and unconventional ways. Elijah was well on his way toward graduation. Although he did not know it then, Elijah would soon approach his final graduation. Nevertheless, more remained for him to learn. He had another test to take, from which he would make more significant progress. In the first chapter of 2 Kings, we learn more about Elijah's continuing maturation.

At least three to four years had passed since the Naboth vineyard episode. King Ahab was now dead, and his son Ahaziah was on the throne. Unfortunately, the new king continued the same sinful and godless reign that King Ahab had practiced. "He did evil in the sight of the LORD and walked in the way of his father" (1 Kings 22:52). King Ahaziah "served Baal and worshiped him and provoked the LORD God of Israel to anger" (1 Kings 22:53).

Subsequently, King Ahaziah suffered a physical injury and became ill. The king sought the counsel of the false Baal prophets, asking them whether he would re-cover (2 Kings 1:2).

God spoke to Elijah through an angel, commanding him to deliver a death pronouncement on King Aha-ziah (2 Kings 1:3–4). Elijah was to return to Samaria, where he had previously received death threats from King Ahab's wife, Queen Jezebel. King Ahab's family was not fond of Elijah, and they welcomed an oppor-tunity to fulfill Queen Jezebel's wish for Elijah's death.

However, this chapter tells of Elijah's complete trust in the Lord. Previously, Elijah had fled from Samaria to Beersheba after Jezebel's death threat (1 Kings 19:3). But now Elijah did not resist God's command to return there. The Scripture states, "Elijah departed" (2 Kings 1:4). Elijah had experienced God's power and faithful-ness many times before. He now felt secure in God's protection and fully empowered to do God's will.

Elijah was sitting on a hill when King Ahaziah's sol-diers confronted him. Interestingly, the king recognized Elijah by the description of his physical appearance and clothing. Elijah had not changed his constitution, even though he was not welcome in this pagan society. As a representative of God, he does not compromise his personality or testimony to become more socially acceptable.

The king wanted a personal meeting with Elijah because he sought a more favorable prognosis for his illness. To ensure this, the king sent fifty men to intimidate and pressure Elijah. Elijah did not yield to such human pressure but responded with an example of God's power. Still, the king did not relent and sent another military force of fifty men, emphasizing an even greater need for Elijah to come immediately. Again, Elijah refused to be intimidated and once again relied on God's power for his safety. Nevertheless, the king was relentless and desperate. So, the king sent yet a third delegation, hoping to persuade Elijah.

God told Elijah to go with that group of soldiers. Their captain had shown humility and reverence for God's power. So Elijah accompanied the soldier and informed the king that God's word for him would not change, regardless of the king's intimidating tactics and desires.

Elijah did not yield to threats, dangers, fears, or any other persuasive force when it came to obeying God. This is a powerful example for Christians to practice when faced with worldly intimidation and the temptation to rebel against God and His Word.

God used Elijah to pronounce a fatal judgment on King Ahaziah for consulting pagan prophets. Messengers delivered Elijah's message and said, "Therefore you shall not come down from the bed where you have gone up, but shall surely die" (2 Kings 1:6). To put it mildly, King Ahaziah was displeased with that prediction. He was also not pleased with Elijah, whom the king learned had pronounced the fatal prophecy.

The king summoned Elijah to appear before the king's court. To ensure Elijah's appearance, the king dispatched three groups of armed soldiers — each containing fifty soldiers — to forcibly bring Elijah to the palace. Fire summoned from Heaven by Elijah destroyed the first two groups. After the third group's leader pleaded humbly with Elijah, Elijah allowed him to take him to the palace. But Elijah did not lessen or change the word of God. Instead, he told the king straight to his face that he would die (2 Kings 1:16).

We see a clear example of Elijah's courage and sense of peace, along with a lack of anxiety, fear, or hesitancy. Elijah did not turn and flee as he had done when threatened by Queen Jezebel. This time, he patiently waited to hear God's instructions. Upon receiving them, he fearlessly proceeded, despite the dangerous situation before him.

We should also note that Elijah delivered God's message *verbatim et literatim*. (Compare 1 Kings 1:3–4, 6, 16.) Elijah did not alter or soften God's message, hoping to lessen his own dangerous position and placate the king.

Whenever we confront an unbeliever, we should always speak the word of God accurately and clearly. That remains true, regardless of the environment or situation. Such courage and obedience indicate we comply with God's University's syllabus.

The hill classroom was the final exam for Elijah. Over the years, God had trained His servant well. Elijah was now thoroughly equipped to complete any task the Lord might assign. Elijah returned to the same palace in Samaria where he first began his ministry. He knew Queen Jezebel was still alive, and the bounty on his head was still in effect. The place he was going was rife with idols, pagan people, and other insidious attendants. Yet, he moved with courage and completed his task.

Elijah learned some lessons from this experience. The first entailed spiritual discernment. He learned to determine with whom he should travel. He also recognized those who wanted to harm him.

The second involved courage. Elijah relied on God's strength and power to enter the presence of his enemies and address them boldly.

Elijah's third lesson entailed trusting God. He believed God would deliver him through a difficult trial in a dangerous setting.

Fourth, Elijah learned about ability. He was given the power, courage, and strength to pronounce God's Word exactly as the Lord intended.

Finally, Elijah experienced God's peace. He knew God had foretold what would happen to King Ahab's dynasty. But Elijah did not ask God for King Ahaziah's deliverance or condemnation. Instead, Elijah peacefully accepted God's divine judgment.

We, too, must develop the virtues of discernment, courage, trust, ability, and peace. However, none of these virtues come quickly or automatically. Instead, we must intentionally cultivate them through our various life trials. The classrooms in which Elijah received his instruction still exist, although not in the exact location or form.

Each Christian should also learn the same lessons Elijah learned. God is immutable. His methods may vary as He chooses, but His curriculum does not. Therefore, if we are serious about our Christian maturity, we must prepare to learn from our individual providential classroom experiences. If we do, it will be one of our most exciting, challenging, and enjoyable experiences.

Insights for Reflection

As an upperclassman student, I saw how my various studies fit with purpose and understanding. Before this stage in my development, I felt there was little or no connection. Each was an individual study and did not relate to my other subjects. A significant turning point occurred when I could answer a test question using the knowledge I had gained from another course.

It also seemed God was again testing me with the same problems I had faced earlier and on which, at the time, I had not performed well. Moreover, many of the new problems I addressed were variations of the old ones, although now modified slightly. Could I, as a senior, now integrate all the education I had gained throughout my college career into a cohesive and complete knowledge of an entire subject?

As mentioned earlier, one of my tragedies was losing some dreams. One of those was a plan my wife and I had to retire and enjoy our sunset years on a beautiful Caribbean island. We had worked long and hard to make that dream a reality. For many years, we saved the needed funds, purchased the empty land, and slowly built our dream home on the ocean in the Bahamas. We finally finished building and furnishing our new home, praying for God's blessing on this project from its inception. Finally, we set our move-in date. I sold my business, and we found a new church ministry in the Bahamas and were ready to make the final transition.

Then it happened. A Category 5 hurricane passed directly over our new home and demolished it. We were heartbroken. All those years of sacrifice and effort were gone in an instant. Like Elijah, I sat on my own little hill of despair and wondered why we now had to deal with such an overwhelming life struggle again. What purpose did God have in allowing such devastation to occur?

Such things can be disheartening if not understood from the proper perspective. Mother Teresa said, "I have never had clarity. What I have always had is trust." Imagine being a soldier on the battlefield and having just shot an enemy, only to see him rise and attack you. You keep shooting. He falls, but rises yet again and continues to come at you. You would wonder if your ammunition or eyes were bad. Perhaps this enemy was invincible. You could easily think the battle was hopeless and that you should surrender.

Elijah had faced King Ahab's family in battle multiple times. As a student, some problems never seem to go away. They are always a hurdle for us to overcome. This also seemed to be Elijah's final test before graduation. Could he unite all the lessons he had learned to address and conquer a new challenge?

One of the health issues I have struggled with is my heart. I was diagnosed with coronary artery disease (CAD) several years ago. Since its inception, I have had twelve stints placed in several of my heart arteries and suffered a heart attack. This issue remains despite the various medical treatments and changes in my physical activities.

I wish this problem would disappear, but it does not lower my commitment to serving Christ. Nor does it interfere with my hearing and understanding God's plan for my life. God's ways are not our ways.

Our worst days are never so bad that we are beyond the grace of God, and our best days are never so good that we do not need the grace of God. Even though some problems seem to remain, and although some issues may repeat themselves, they do not change our immutable God and should never minimize how much we love and trust Him.

In these times, it may appear we are not making progress, mainly when an event seems to reoccur. We may even fail some of these repetitive tests, but we should not give up. Our God is a faithful and patient teacher who does not intend to leave any devoted student with a failing grade. So, do not become disheartened if you repeat a test. Instead, if you remain faithful to pursue God and obey Him, you will experience victory.

Questions

1. Elijah's faith was strengthened by the numerous times he experienced God's power, provisions, protection, and personal communication. What specific events in your life have you experienced where similar manifestations from God have helped to fortify your faith?

2. Why do you think God continually tests our faith, even when we have repeatedly shown our trust and allegiance to Him?

3. How should Christians prepare and respond when pressured to enter an unsafe arena with dangerous people?

CLASS 401
Fire from Heaven

(Graduation)

"And it came about when the LORD was about to take up Elijah by a whirlwind to heaven, that Elijah went with Elisha from Gilgal. Elijah said to Elisha, 'Stay here please, for the LORD has sent me as far as Bethel.' But Elisha said, 'As the LORD lives and as you yourself live, I will not leave you. So they went down to Bethel. Then the sons of the prophets who [were at] Bethel came out to Elisha and said to him, 'Do you know that the LORD will take away your master from over you today?' And he said, 'Yes, I know; be still.' Elijah said to him, 'Elisha, please stay here, for the LORD has sent me to Jericho.' But he said, As the LORD lives, and as you yourself live, I will not leave you.' So they came to Jericho. The sons of the prophets who [were] at Jericho approached Elisha and said to him, 'Do you know that the LORD will take away

your master from over you today?' And he answered, 'Yes, I know; be still.' Then Elijah said to him, 'Please stay here, for the LORD has sent me to the Jordan.' And he said, 'As the LORD lives, and as you yourself live, I will not leave you.' So the two of them went on. Now fifty men of the sons of the prophets went and stood opposite [them] at a distance, while the two of them stood by the Jordan. Elijah took his mantle and folded it together and struck the waters, and they were divided here and there, so that the two of them crossed over on dry ground. When they had crossed over, Elijah said to Elisha, 'Ask what I shall do for you before I am taken from you.' And Elisha said, 'Please, let a double portion of your spirit be upon me.' He said, 'You have asked a hard thing. [Nevertheless,] if you see me when I am taken from you, it shall be so for you; but if not, it shall not be [so].' As they were going along and talking, behold, [there appeared] a chariot of fire and horses of fire which separated the two of them. And Elijah went up by a whirlwind to heaven (2 Kings 2:1–11).

The objective of this class is to inspect our current level of spiritual growth, faith, humility, love, and obedience to Christ Jesus.

Elijah's story did not end when he delivered the prophecy of King Ahaziah's death. Instead, Scripture says Elijah went directly to Heaven after completing his earthly ministry. What a graduation. To finish his godly service on earth, to leave a legacy admired by all, and to be succeeded by a man who would continue his work was an honor unparalleled in this world. Elijah's reward dwarfs any medal or prize others might give us. The many classroom lessons, trials, and sufferings Elijah experienced pale in significance to the honor he received in the end.

The final chapter of Elijah's life shows that he visited several meaningful geographical areas, starting with Gilgal and including Bethel, Jericho, and the Jordan. These areas were significant and benefited Elijah's companion and successor, Elisha.

Looking at these locations from our university student perspective, we remember Bethel, which means house of God, was where Jacob experienced his dream about God as he began his spiritual journey. Here, Jacob stood in the presence of Almighty God. Jacob also received the promises of God for his future here. As Elijah journeyed to Bethel, he may also have recalled the vision he received from God and how God had likewise made promises concerning the future of his godly mission.

Every student in God's University has once received a calling — an idea of what God wanted that student to do. They have also received in some way an assurance that God would be with them through all the trials and lessons they would encounter along the way.

Jericho was known as an impregnable city (2 Kings 2:4). Although it seemingly could not be conquered, Jericho fell before the godly power of Joshua's attacking army. Perhaps, Elijah reflected on that conquest when he stood on Mt. Carmel. His enemies were also proud and confident of their imminent victory. But yet again, God demonstrated that the efforts of people could not match His will.

As Christian students approaching graduation, we can look at the many daunting spiritual battles we have faced as we pursue God. There were times when our enemy appeared stronger, more determined, and invincible. We were weak and without resources to prevail. The outcome was sometimes questionable, and our faith may have wavered. Ultimately, however, we won our battles through God's power. Just as in the days of Elijah, God proved to be true and reliable.

When Elijah was at Bethel and Jericho, the prophets demonstrated their awareness of Elijah's upcoming departure from earth and that a whirlwind would take him to heaven (2 Kings 2:1). The works Elijah had performed, and his coming graduation, were known to many, but not to all. And so it is also true of us. Although the world may not know of a faithful Christian's work, God's people possess knowledge and appreciation of that person's labor.

Finally, Elijah reached the Jordan River. Here, Elijah performed his final miracle. Elijah took off his cloak, rolled it up, and struck the waters. Immediately, the water parted, allowing Elijah and Elisha to cross safely (2 Kings 2:8).

After crossing the Jordan River, Elijah asked Elisha what he could do for him before God took him to heaven. Elisha's answer was most unusual and unexpected. Elisha did not want money or power. Instead, he only asked that a double portion of Elijah's spirit be given to him (2 Kings 2:9).

Elijah told Elisha he had asked for a hard thing (2

Kings 2:10a). But why would he say that? Was it difficult or impossible for Elijah to grant his request? No, because God would grant the request, not Elijah. And God is all-powerful. Instead, the reluctance lay within Elijah, who was painfully aware of the many difficult trials and sufferings he had endured to mature in his faith. Now, Elisha wished to take on the heavy burden of such a journey and to make it doubly more difficult and painful.

Elijah wanted Elisha to recognize that his journey would be difficult if God granted him his wish. We may look back and speculate that Elijah said the following to Elisha: "Elisha, do you understand the misery and suffering and pain and agony that might accompany such a request?"

As mature believers counsel immature believers, we should inform them about the difficult challenges Christians face as they grow in their faith. Many new believers mistakenly think their lives will suddenly become perfect when they believe. Following Christ is not easy, and difficult trials will come. Recall the words of Christ in John 16:33, "These things I have spoken to you, so that in Me you may have peace. In the world you have tribulation, but take courage; I have overcome the world."

Also, recall Paul's warning in 2 Timothy 3:12: "Indeed, all who desire to live godly in Christ Jesus will be persecuted." Paul did not equivocate but was emphatic that believers will endure some form of persecution.

To review, I would like to summarize Elijah's life and juxtapose it with the words of Paul as recorded in 2 Timothy 4:7, "I have fought the good fight, I have finished the course, I have kept the faith."

Elijah fought with Ahab and Jezebel, among others. Yet, he remained firm in his faith and obedient, following his God-ordained path. He fought the good fight and stayed on course. Like Paul, he finished well. But unlike Paul, Elijah experienced a unique graduation ceremony. We will probably not have an earthly transition like Elijah, but like Paul and Elijah, we are fighting the good fight, we are on a designated course, and we should keep the faith. Our goal should entail finishing well and hearing God say, "Well done."

Insights for Reflection

As I write this, I am sitting at my desk and working

on a lesson for my Sunday adult Bible study class. Winter is approaching here in northern Ohio. The leaves have fallen, and the first snowfall has occurred. The days are short, dark, and cold. Yet, I am looking at a beautiful photo of a Caribbean island and wondering where my wife and I might be had that hurricane not destroyed our dream retirement home.

Am I bitter? Not really. Sadness? That is another story. But I also have a profound sense of peace and contentment. Over time, I have accepted that setback as a part of God's will. We did not plan or desire this. Yet I see more clearly now that our retirement at that place was not as important as we thought. We now look to our ultimate retirement, and my wife and I look to the day of glory we can call our final graduation.

Graduation is the day all students eagerly anticipate. Finally, what was once so far off arrives. Graduation is when all the energy, time, and sacrifices become worthwhile. We can stop studying and put our books down for good. We can relax and enjoy the fruits of our labor.

But is that true? Can a Christian ever say our education is over in this life? Can a believer ever say God has taught them all they need to know to serve in their chosen ministries? No, our graduation will not occur until we leave this earth. But, even then, we should not view that graduation as final. God is an infinite being and cannot ever be completely known.

We are currently in the sanctification phase of our salvation, having been justified by the atoning works of Jesus Christ on the cross. The Holy Spirit teaches us more about our Lord daily as we submit to His guidance. While we will be evaluated and rewarded for our faithfulness, coming to a complete knowledge of the Almighty God is an ongoing process.

Elijah left earth, but Scripture does not say his work ended. We later see Elijah appear on the Mount of Transfiguration with Jesus (Matthew 17:3, Mark 9:4). Many also believe Elijah is one of the two witnesses who will return to earth in its final days during the Tribulation (Revelation 11).

Our individual study of almighty God will continue regardless of our view concerning Elijah's departure. God is eternal and omniscient. No one on earth can ever fully comprehend God, regardless of how much time and effort they devote to that undertaking. Our intelligence is limited. We can only admire God's brilliance and hope to learn more about His attributes.

But this should not frustrate us because every time we study, we learn more about God and grow closer to Him. We are His children, and we share in His incredible love. That is the greatest reward we can receive from our many studies. Therefore, student, press on in your godly scholarship. Do not think your graduation day at God's University will never come. Think only that it will never end.

Peace be on all of God's students, and blessings to you all!

Questions

1. Are you pleased with your current progress toward spiritual maturity? If not, why not? Why do you think God gave Elijah such a unique transition into Heaven?

2. Elisha wanted a double portion of Elijah's spirit. Would you ask God for such spiritual power if you knew you would face tremendous adversities? Why would you want to make such a request? What makes you think you could handle what the fulfillment of such a request would bring?

Appendix

I have used Elijah as an appropriate subject for a student enrolled in God's University. But we should not limit enrollment in this school based on having a personality or a family upbringing like Elijah's.

The Bible illustrates many individuals enrolled in and subject to God's curriculum to develop sound wisdom and full spiritual maturity. One example is the patriarch Job, who underwent a period of isolation not unlike Elijah's experience at the brook of Cherith (Class 101). Job experienced depressing loneliness when his wife and best friends turned against the God whom Job worshipped and relied on. None of them offered Job any empathy or support in his time of need. Instead, they influenced Job so much that he eventually questioned God and sought answers but received only silence.

In Genesis, Joseph is another example of a person thrust into solitude and retreat. He was cut off from his family for many years. I am sure Joseph longed for the familiar smiling faces of his loved ones, but he only received negativity in a brutal environment.

Abraham is yet another example. He was called

away from his parental homeland and instructed by God to give up the life he led and move to distant lands.

In the Zarephath class (102), Elijah had to rely on a foreign woman for daily nutrients and survival. In the Bible, we also read of individuals such as Rahab, the harlot, and Ruth, who found themselves in dire straits and forced to depend upon foreigners for survival.

In Class 201, where we studied the fire on Mt. Carmel, Elijah's faith was on public display. Likewise, we read of the three Hebrew boys Shadrach, Meshach, and Abed-nego in Daniel 12. They were given a life-and-death ultimatum to prove the truth of their faith in a public setting. But they stood firm in their faith and successfully demonstrated to King Nebuchadnezzar that their God was mightier than the pagan king's command and his gods. Also, we see a similar example in Daniel when his willingness to be thrown into the lion's den brilliantly illustrated the full depth of his faith.

In the Mt. Horeb class (202), Elijah struggled with depression. Similarly, we read about the Apostle Paul and his companions in 2 Corinthians 1:8. They were so burdened and overcome that they despaired even of life. Such a severe and overwhelming depression is not uncommon among believers, as demonstrated by Moses, Jonah, and David.

In the vineyard class (301), we read about Elijah and his return to King Ahab's homestead. A similar narrative would be the example of Joshua, a man who, in his old age, had to fight again an enemy with whom he had tangled earlier in his life. The biblical narrative of the two-fold battle in Joshua chapters 7 and 8 illustrates God urging Joshua to overcome his fears and face his enemy once again.

In Class 302, we read of God commissioning Elijah for another confrontation with a pagan king. In the Bible, we find many examples of God placing His people in difficult situations where they must face their enemies. Jesus' disciples found that serving God led them into battle with human and evil celestial beings.

Admission to God's University is one of the highest honors anyone could receive. This education is not an easy schooling, nor is it one that operates under a human schedule. God is its president, college dean, athletic coach, and personal tutor. He avails Himself to each student at any time through prayer. He decides what test each student must take and when. God alone assesses each student's progress and spiritual maturity level. And, of course, God alone gives each student a personal final grade.

All these positions may appear too mysterious to comprehend, and perhaps even harsh and cruel. Nevertheless, the one goal every student hopes to achieve is to see the university president extend his hand and hold a diploma for them to receive.

That final graduation ceremony does not occur for believers in this life. Instead, it comes later when we leave this earth to meet the Lord. At that time, our Lord will extend His welcoming hand and say "Well done" to all who graduate at the Judgment Seat (Bema) of Christ (2 Corinthians 5:10, 2 Timothy 2:5).

A good verse to memorize is James 1:12: "Blessed is a man who perseveres under trials; for once he has been approved, he will receive the crown of life which the Lord has promised those who love Him."

I pray that you will be a dedicated student at God's University. Be attentive, learn, share, remain committed, and stay in class.

Blessings to all who are enrolled in God's University!

Biography

Edward C. Morris is a native of New Orleans, Louisiana. He resides in the Akron, Ohio, area. He teaches theology in his local church and small adult groups. He is also a former lay leader in the Coast Guard Auxiliary.

He holds a bachelor of science degree in electrical engineering from Southern University in Baton Rouge, Louisiana. He also holds a master's degree in theological studies from Malone University in Canton, Ohio.

He is married to Brenda Lee and is blessed to have two children, daughter Rhonda (Morris) Wilson and her husband Shawn, (parents to grandchildren Joshua and David Wilson), and son Daniel Morris.

He enjoys family time, sailing and gardening.

Endnotes

1 Arthur W. Pink, *The Life of Elijah*, (Grand Rapids, MI. Zondervan Publishing), 40.

2 *Ibid*, 93.

3 William A. Vangemeren, *Interpreting the Prophetic Word* (Academic Books, Grand Rapids, MI. Zondervan Publishing, 1990).

4 Simon J. DeVries, *World Biblical Commentary* (Volume 12) (Waco, Texas World Books, 1985).

5 F. W. Krummacher, *Elijah the Tishbite* (Grand Rapids, MI. Zondervan Publishing), 120– 121. "Here the whole miraculous history of the ancient fathers would revive before him in the liveliest colors. Fresh images and scenes from that age of wonders would recur to his mind at every step, and the very profound silence around him would assist in the consideration of the sublime things, at which these spots had been once the theater. As often as he descended into a green and palmy vale, he alighted in spirit on some resting place of his fathers. As often as the shade of an overhanging rock received him, it was as if the incense of the sanctuary breathed around him; for the prayers of the pilgrims of God had hollowed these shades. Here or there, he would think, perhaps Moses had rested and taken counsel in the sacred circle of his elders; and the leader of Israel was still seen kneeling before the Lord, and speaking to Him, and then 'as a man talketh with his friend.' Thus one heart-elating thought would follow another. The history of the forty year's journey would attain a form and a vitality beyond what he had hitherto realized. At one time he would seem to be gathering the manna with the ancient fathers; at another to be standing with the wounded before the

brazen image of the serpent and feeling with them the return of health. Presently he would be in spirit at the altar which Moses built and called it 'Jehovah Nissi' the Lord my banner; and then again would hear the desert resound with loud thanksgiving and solemn hymns of praise to the faithfulness and truth of Jehovah. Every new scene on which he entered, would bring before him some new event and feature of those journeying which were irradiated with the Glory of God; and whatever consolation and encouragement is comprised in these histories, would rush upon him with sublime and overwhelming wonder, or exhilarate him with a spring of hope and joy, that seemed to give wings to his feet, and banish the last remains of fear and care from his spirit."

6 William Taylor, *Elijah the Prophet*, (New York Harper & Brothers, 1875) 154.

7 *Ibid*, 156.

8 Reverend Michael Lawrence, *Biblical Theology*, (Wheaton, Illinois Crossway Publishing, 2010).

9 William Taylor, *Ibid*, 155.